Parenting By Faith

(Good Parenting Matters...
My Children are The Proof!)

Louise A. Battle
(Best Selling Author)

Foreword by Ernestine Allen,
2011 National Mother of the Year

Xulon
PRESS

Parenting By Faith
(Good Parenting Matters...My Children are The Proof!)
by Louise A. Battle

Printed in the United States of America

ISBN 9781498426633

Telephone numbers, addresses, web sites and offers listed in this book are accurate at the time of publication, but may be subject to change.

Bible quotations are taken interchangeably from The King James Version (KJV), The New International Version (NIV) and The New American Standard Version (NASV) from the Comparative Study Bible. Copyright © 1984 by The Zondervan Corporation.

www.xulonpress.com

ATTENTION: Hospitals, Churches, Schools, Businesses and
Parenting Advocates

Books are available at quantity discounts with bulk purchase for educational, business, or sales promotional use. For information, please contact Lbattlenolonger@hotmail.com or write to:

Reverend Louise A. Battle
Special Sales
P. O. Box 1243
Landover, Maryland 20785

As the Author of this Book...

I am declaring to the heavens that every angel in heaven that belongs to me, to the prince of the air and to every demon in hell....that my children, all of their children, my step children, all of their children, my spiritual children, all of their children, my grand-children, all of their children and
Every

child of all the parents I teach and children of those who read this book.......be snatched from the hands of the enemy to enable <u>all</u> of these children to be trained to serve God and fulfill their purpose and the plan that God has laid out for their lives,
In Jesus Name!

I declare and decree it to be so, and so it is done!

Parents, I wrote this book for you!

I deserved a Great son and a Great daughter, so I put in the work and I got them both! God and his angels have and still are a constant and present help at all times.

I have truly enjoyed writing this book! Remember, Love Lets Go! This book is dedicated to God, who enabled me to write it and allow so many lives to be touched and enriched.

Acknowledgements

Appreciation goes to every professor who taught me at The Howard University School of Divinity in the late 1990's; especially to Dean Clarence Newsome, the former Dean, who touched my life simply by teaching and directing me. The best way to describe the atmosphere at the Howard University School of Divinity is simple: A Family! I am forever grateful!

Appreciation also goes to the late, Ms. Alma Hawkins, my former business teacher at Randall Jr. High School in Southwest D. C. who taught me how to type. Typing this manuscript was a labor of love. Many thanks to Nekida Burns and Dora Stuart for their expertise in assisting me in completing this project, Parenting By Faith, initially in April of 1997 at the twenty-fourth hour! I will never forget it and I am eternally grateful! Special appreciation goes to my five excellent Editors; daughter, April K. Oliver, son, Phillip A. Oliver, sister, Carolyn V. Marbley, dearest friend and writing mentor, Dr. Barbara Reynolds and co-worker Charlene Baker for editing this book!

My prayer is that everyone who reads this would be touched, eyes opened, strengthened and ministered to by the Holy Spirit. To the Great Threesome, my God, Jesus and the Holy Spirit; I give all the glory, honor, credit and praise for guiding, directing and ordering my steps as a parent to raise the fruit of my womb with a faith that never broke, nor bended in the belief that my children would always belong to the threesome. I can see the manifestation of it all from their fruitful lives. My prayers, tears and challenges raising them during the younger years of their lives as a single parent because of their father's death were not in vain. God did for me what my deceased husband could not....He helped me snatch them from the hands of the enemy many, many times! To God, I give <u>All</u> the credit!

Dedication

This book is also dedicated to my mother and first teacher, the late Naomi E. Young, from whom I learned how to parent and who possessed an infinite and absolute amount of determination since the birth of my sister, Carolyn and I, that we would be somebody! She passed that determination to us, to inspire our own children. Also to my late husband and best friend, Frank C. Oliver, Jr. whose last words to me were, "Louise, I Love You, take care of my children and get some bass in your voice."

Also dedicated to the two jewels; our children, from which our union of Love, matrimony, and passion brought forth; April and Phillip. To my sister, Carolyn, whom we have shared parenting skills through the years and prayed together over many of those *"creative"* parenting skills! I thank God for the warrior father and mother figures who were in place to assist me in raising my son and daughter through prayer, babysitting, physically taking them under their wings; by spending time with them, assisting financially, providing food, advice, guidance or whatever was needed for their nurturing and development. Those seeds planted, have groomed them to become the man and woman that they are today.

It took a village and the village is as follows: The late James and Frances Bolden, (my God-parents), Pastor Grant Russell, (friend and warrior prayer partner), the late Catherine Gist, (precious friend of our family), the late Carlton Simenton, (my cousin), the late Walter Battle, (my uncle), Ralph Battle, (my uncle), James Shelton (my cousin), Special thanks to Mr. Cardell Shelton, (former employer, friend and community activist), the late Mr. Shaar Mustaf, (Founder and Director of The Take Charge Program), Mr. Frank Banner, (Director of the Shepherding Mentoring Program) and both Mr. Alfred Mitchell and Mr. Cunningham who were advocates for our youth in the Maryland area; Bishop David T. P. Perrin, Pastors Joshua K. White and Terri White, the late Brother Graham and his wife, Meleasa and many of the members of my former church family, Church of the Great Commission, Pastor Deron Cloud, the Oliver Family, Marlin and Amy Peters, the late Gail Peters, Betty Peters, Vanessa Majors, Alma Boone, Shirley Turner, Carolyn Harvey, Sheila Hull, Reverend Belindia Boyer, my current neighbors: Minnie Battle and Reverend Porter Lawson; my church family at my former church, First

Baptist Church of Albuquerque, New Mexico; Pastor Joe McKinney, Naomi Jones and her daughter, NaTanya Jones, the late Dennis Lithe; Pastors Richard and Christine Dunk at The Living Word Fellowship in Fredericksburg, Virginia; Barbara Causey, Bobby and Rose Foster of Albuquerque, New Mexico; the late Alma Winters and her daughter, the late Jean Winters; Pastors Shine and Dee Dee at the former Save the Seed Program, the Scared Straight Program at the former Lorton Penitentiary in Lorton, Virginia and former Pastors of New Life Assembly in Capitol Heights, Maryland, Mike and Kay Zello. Thank you, I Love and appreciate all of you so very much!

> *"Train up a child in the way he should go, even when he is old, he will not depart." Proverbs 22:6*

Foreword

❝I am especially grateful and honored for being asked to write this Foreword. This is an excellent "How To" parenting book. Elder Louise Battle has written several books, but certainly this one tops them all! After reading this well written book, I know it will be a blessing to young parents as well as single mothers and fathers. It is an easy read and a wonderful guide for parenting. Elder Battle certainly has covered each step needed in raising children.

There is a serious struggle today with working moms, young moms and those who become pregnant as teenagers. So many of our children are having children and if you think parenting is difficult, think how much harder it is when you are just a child yourself. "Many young parents have failed miserably in their struggle to raise a child for which they were unprepared. However, many have been successful because they have had an extra-large dose of help, compassion and wisdom. It all came from people who cared too much to let them fail," eloquently stated by Bishop T. D. Jakes.

"Parenting By Faith" is a very appropriate title for this book, mainly because we can't see around the corners of our lives. Parenting brings many challenges as well as disappointments. It would be my ultimate desire to live a long life to continue enjoying my two sons and grandchildren. However, the sad time for me being a parent, was to actually lose my youngest son to death. My entire life was impacted because this was out of order. Children should bury their parents, not parents burying their children. This is the time you really need faith to parent. At some point or the other, all parents are faced with the decision of, "do I continue or quit?" This comes to your mind, even if it's just a fleeting thought.

This book will be especially helpful to so many parents who perhaps do not have a firm belief system and Christian values in which to teach to their children. Elder Battle takes a step by step approach to parenting and this book is a true guide to parenting by faith. If parenting is your major concern, then God certainly will perfect it. The Bible tells us that "He will perfect that which concerns me." Psalm 138:8

I have been encouraged reading this wonderful, well written and thought out Bible based book and will recommend it to parents as well as single moms. I did not realize the true impact parents had on their children, especially moms until I was nominated as the "2011 National Mother of the Year." It opened many doors of opportunities for me to speak to parents and single mothers. After traveling to several states including Puerto Rico, I am persuaded that all parents face the same dilemma in parenting. The most challenging question with so many parents today and especially young parents is "Am I doing it right?" This book demonstrates to us, how it is done!

Finally, Elder Battle teaches us how strong the power of encouragement is to our children. More children succeed through encouragement than criticism. Parenting By Faith is an amazing book for all. I pray God will take Elder Battle to heights unknown as this book reaches the masses across the country."

Mother Ernestine Allen
Greater Mount Calvary Holy Church
Washington, D. C.

Table Of Contents

1

Introduction

Throughout history, it has always been said that children are a blessing from God. This book attempts to bring together my experiences and the research of many scholars who have written on the issues of parenting, to give parents a plan to strengthen their faith and skills. Therefore, parents will be able to raise children whose lives reflect maturity, caring and the ability to take care of themselves, yet display understanding and compassion for others. Raising children whose faith is in Jesus Christ.

We will first explore in Section I, the purpose of parents and their role. Raising children will deeply affect, change and touch your life in a way that you will never be the same. Never will a job teach you so much, stretch you so far, command you to examine yourself, keep you on your knees praying and keep you constantly, continuously and daily, moment by moment dependent on God.

Never will a job assist you in experiencing your emotions to the point where at times, you feel completely helpless and on the other hand, at other times, feel like you are in total control. As a parent, in comparison to the grades of a government employee; sometimes your parenting skill level is at the grade level of a GS-2 and at other times, you will feel like your parenting skill level is at the grade level of a GS-15.

Section II will outline the developmental stages of children beginning at infancy, birth to crawling or walking to late adolescence, ages 16-21. This outline is an effort to share what happens during those developmental stages, so that the challenging tasks of raising children is made a little easier and equips the parent(s) with understanding.

Scriptures are used throughout this book to enlighten and ignite the faith of parents to "Live the Word." Faith is the foundation in raising children and this subject will be coupled with the issue of discipline. The American Heritage® Dictionary of the English Language, Fifth Edition. Copyright © 2011 by Houghton Mifflin Harcourt Publishing Company; published by Houghton Mifflin Harcourt Publishing Company defines discipline as,

"Training expected to produce a specific type or patterns of behavior, especially training that produces moral or mental improvement."

Discipline is not only punishment; parents must know what to say and what to do. It is obvious in our world today that parents need help. Many parents justify their current parenting practices by saying that when they had their children, they did not come with a manual. They did not know what to do. But just as we study Mathematics, English/Spelling and get degrees in specific areas to pursue our careers; parents must study how to be a parent. Section III will concentrate on the issue of educating parents and present a strategic plan for parenting workshops.

Many times, situations arise in families and parents do not know how to handle them. Section III will also present several questions and answers pertaining to areas of children's developmental stages answered by Dr. James Dobson and Dr. Peter Favaro.

In summary and conclusion, parents will be reminded of what the Scriptures say about raising our children. This book is important because children need models of good parenting.

2

My Story

As a young girl, I always dreamed of planning a wedding, marrying a tall, fine, Black man; going to Paris, France to get married, settle down in Washington, D. C., and later have a daughter and son.

You are probably saying, "That girl is dreaming big time." I was. I use to read a lot as a young girl about far away places, like Paris, France, Rome and Spain and always wanted to travel to those beautiful places. The breath-taking pictures in the books assisted me in desiring to visit those places. Let's face it......some women will read that and say, "That's my testimony too!" Well, two out of three is not bad. I did marry the tall, fine, Black man, Frank and I did have the girl and boy, April and Phillip. Paris has not been fulfilled, YET!

I have visited Rome, different parts of France and Spain, but did not get married there!

Being a mother was always a part of my plan for my life. I dreamed of raising children who would not only touch my life, but would touch the lives of other people in the world. Years before our children were conceived; Frank and I spent hours, talking all the time. We talked about our individual and corporate goals and dreams, our upbringing in our families, our future together and especially having and raising our children. I wrote on paper, what we wanted each of our children exposed to, the deposits we wanted to directly make in our children's lives, knowledge of specific places and experiences that we wanted them to have.

Frank directed me to write it all down as we spoke about it. It was mainly Frank who had the specific deposits he wanted made in our unborn children's lives and he was serious! I felt such an outpouring of love for him and our not yet conceived and unborn children when we discussed this! Frank was 12 years older than I and had several children from previous marriages and relationships before we met. I highly respected his wisdom, knowledge and experience. You are probably saying, marrying a man with several children, it did not matter because I was deeply "in love" with him. I am moving ahead of myself, with a specific purpose in mind; I felt that background information was needed. Frank and I took the Lamaze classes together. Lamaze is an international company that offers classes and promotes a natural, healthy and safe approach to pregnancy, childbirth and early parenting practices. Lamaze classes taught us about what to expect and what choices are available during childbirth. Frank took pictures in the delivery room as he saw the birth of our first child, April, delivered by a mid-wife in the hospital in Albuquerque, New Mexico! He was nervous, so many of the pictures reflect it. Frank had never seen the birth of any of his previous children! It was a fantastic, memorable experience for both of us…I enjoyed being pregnant!

Frank would tie my shoes, because I could not reach them, rub my stomach with a cream called, "Mother's Friend," he gave me baths, always washing my back and then tenderly helped me out of the bathtub, fixed breakfast and dinner, ran with me while I was pregnant, (I was in the military while carrying April); gave me massages and rubbed my feet. Frank drove to Dunkin Donuts every time I craved donuts and went with me to all of my doctor's appointments. I desired to have another child for Frank because I truly enjoyed being pregnant and I especially enjoyed making love with him!

I still have the yellow sheets of legal paper of the planned experiences for our children *before* we had our children and will share many of those experiences in this book and others in my upcoming parenting classes/workshops. It will give you examples of many of our desires for our children. We pre-planned for our children and wanted both of our children to master four specific areas, *reading, writing, mathematics and speaking*! Frank would always tell me that if they mastered these four, they would have an edge on life and there would be nothing that they could not accomplish. He was correct! It may sound simple, but we wanted each of our children to experience a ride on a boat, a horse, a train, and an airplane as a child. They both have had all of the above experiences as a child.

I remember both of my children's first experience riding on a horse. It was in Albuquerque, New Mexico during the time I was a missionary in Albuquerque, New Mexico and my funds were tight. April was 13 and Phillip was 8 years old. I had $40.00 extra this particular month and wanted them to have the experience. The cost was $15.00 for each one to ride for 30 minutes. I wanted so bad to ride with them, but did not have enough money. I sat, watched them and enjoyed every moment of their experience. They connected with those horses…it made my heart feel so happy!

All of the things we wrote down prior to April and Phillip being conceived have been accomplished! Writing them down, kept the goals before us and especially helped me to continue to focus on them after the passing of Frank in 1989 to be with the Lord. The fact that *I wrote* them down.... they were always in my head! Our children loved to write......they got that from my DNA and both loved to talk.....they got that from Frank's DNA! They both wrote poems when they were younger and my son wrote his autobiography at twelve years of age, (112 pages). That summer, I had him to type it into a manuscript along with his poems and we placed it in a binder for future publishing. We still have that binder. Our daughter has authored one book of poetry, entitled, "Girl Talk" and another book of poetry and short stories, entitled, "Boy Talk."

Being a mother is like being a firefighter. You are constantly putting out fires with your hands, with water and sometimes with tissue! This simply means, you are constantly solving problems and helping your children to solve the problems that living life brings. When they are little, you use your hands to hold, hug and love your child. You also use your hands to pray for them and anoint them. You also use your hands to place bandages on real bruises and also on some long-ago healed scars too!

You use water to prevent messes in their lives from getting messier! You try your best to protect them, but in truth. You use tissues to wipe tears away and show them how to lift up their heads and together you go to fight the fires! Parenting is the most challenging and rewarding job I have ever had and the benefits are great! The fruitful lives of my children are the benefits. Grown children give back what you have deposited in them as children. You will either invest the time, energy, patience and money in your children when they are young or you will invest it when they are older. If you do not invest in them when they are younger…you will pay a higher price later! Parents must make the decision and sacrifice as to whether to make the proper deposits in their children and pay now…when they are younger or pay later when they are grown. It is difficult to place basic values and moral principles into grown children that should have been placed in them at a younger age. For example, don't let the schools and their peers be totally responsible for your child's sex education. Sit down and tell your children in simple language, how they were conceived.

My daughter still remembers how I used a condom and rolled it on a hot dog representing a males' penis. I explained the use of a condom to prevent pregnancy to both of my children. She was 12 years old and was not having sex and my son was seven. If you as a parent won't take the time to explain the correct methods, who will? I explained to my children that "Frank and I loved each other. I told both of my children that they were planned for and thought about thoroughly beforehand. I told my children that Daddy and Mommy made love. Daddy placed his private part, his penis in Mommy's private part, her vagina and that is how each of you was conceived. I chose a book specifically written to explain reproduction to a child and showed them the pictures. I did the same above procedure with my grand-children.

Choose a book with pictures to assist you in making it simple, using the proper names for body parts and functions. As quiet as it has been kept, Parents, you are responsible for your child's spiritual development. Do not let _not_ going to church or attending the wrong church develop your child's spirituality!

What do you believe and who will tell them about God, His laws and His precepts, because there is a God! What you as parents do, always speaks louder than what you say.

3

Memory Lane…My…I Remember…When

I *remember when*….I served in the Army at my first assignment as an Officer at the Kirkland Air Force Base in Albuquerque, New Mexico where we lived and was pregnant with our daughter, April. I loved to run/jog and Frank used to run every morning with me until I reached the ninth month. I have always felt that I was in the best physical shape I have ever experienced during that period of my life!

I remember when….I constantly craved Dunkin Donuts while carrying April and there was one about 5 minutes away from where we lived on the Base. Frank was one of their best customers! I remember one evening I had the craving and he decided to buy a dozen donuts instead of purchasing 2 or 3 of my favorite…..maple donuts.

When he woke up the next morning.....there were 3 donuts left of the 12 and he never had one of the nine. He was upset with me and told me so. I ate them all, but did not realize how many I had eaten! They were so good. He never bought me a dozen donuts again!

I remember when....We celebrated holidays as a child. My Mother always made birthdays, Easter and Christmas big and special, special days!

I remember when....Many times, my sister and I would cut up and act like teenagers do. My mother would call our Aunt Rose over and tell her about our behavior. Aunt Rose would place both me and Carolyn in the middle of our living room floor, anoint us both, lay hands on us and pray a powerful, long, long prayer for us.

By the time she finished praying; both me, my sister and my mother would be crying. After the prayer, we would hug our mother and tell her that we will never act up again and we really felt and meant that. We felt and acted like angels for about two weeks and then we would cut up again and Momma would call Aunt Rose over again to do the same thing.

I remember when....My mother sacrificed! When we were younger, my mother owned three suits, a black, blue and brown suit that she interchangeably wore to work so that we could wear beautiful clothes and nice shoes.

I remember when....My mother always had my Uncle Arthur as one of the chaperones for the teenage parties we would have. It was so fun, all of our friends would ask for him when they arrived and the party did not start until he came. At least the dancing did not start until he came. We used to do a dance we called the "slow drag" where the boy and girl stood close to one another, held each other and danced. Uncle Arthur would turn the red bulb off that we had in the ceiling for one second and say….you better get everything you can get and we would all bust out laughing!

Uncle Arthur had no teeth in his mouth, but could eat an apple better than you and me with teeth! It was amazing to watch him eat an apple.

I remember when…..I bought used cars in the earlier lives of my children to make sure my family could move around the city with ease. I always paid less than $600.00 for the cars. Of course, I had to carry water, oil, transmission fluid, brake fluid, window washer and old rags in the trunk of my car at all times because my cars would always on a daily basis, run hot, needing water or needing oil or transmission fluid during my ride from home to my short, within the city destinations. The dealers were less than honest about what was wrong with these cars, even though I knew I was purchasing somebody elses' problem, the price of the cars fit my budget……… they were cheap!

I would bargain with the dealers and get them down as low as I could. I got what I paid

for, however, I learned about cars this way....
unintentionally planned, but thank you very much!

Today, I drive a much better car, but I still carry
the necessary fluids in the trunk of my car and
can open the hood of any car and <u>know</u> where
the oil, transmission fluid, water, window washer
and brake fluid goes!

When we visited my Mother on Sundays for
dinner, she would tell me, "Louise, I heard you
coming down the street before I saw you." I
especially remember a red car I bought that had
a large hole in the back passenger, left hand side
of the floor...I did not realize it until the children
told me they could see the ground as I drove.
I thought they were kidding...they talk and we
laugh about it now and they said, they felt like
members of the cartoons, The Flintstones, with
me driving and their feet sometimes touching
the ground!

The hole was covered by a mat...the dealer
never told me the hole was there. Car dealers
loved to see me coming. Lesson learned: my next
purchase of cars, I looked under all mats to make
sure there were no holes in the floors!

I remember when.....my husband and I
separated for a short period of time during our
marriage and we moved out of our home and I
obtained the cheapest, but affordable apartment
I could find which happened to be located on
Howard Road, S. E., when it was a very rough
area. All the individual houses on the block had

a different color door. After a month or two living there, my apartment was broken into while I was at work and part of my rent money was stolen. I was devastated, angry and felt violated!

There were only 2-3 persons including myself on the block that worked. In fact, one of my neighbors began to baby sit for me when my car broke down and I was unable to get my son to our babysitter who lived across the bridge on the other side of Southeast. My one bedroom apartment had a bathroom attached, but the mice and roaches were so rampant, bold and stayed so visible, I thought they were going to help me with the rent! If you placed a glass of juice on the table or floor for over 5 minutes, by the time you picked the glass back up….it would be full of roaches! They were hungry and opportunists!

When the lights went out…the mice would come out. They made so much noise. I never slept well living on Howard Road. My children slept in the same bed with me, because I felt I had to keep awake to protect them from those noisy mice looking for food.

I remember when….I was so frustrated living on Howard Road that one Sunday after church as I drove my beat-up looking, old, brown car that made the loud noises, and the car in which every hour I had to put water in the radiator as it ran hot; I had decided to ask my Mother to watch my children and take care of them. I had written a letter to the then current Mayor of Washington,

D. C., Mayor Marion Barry and told her that I intended to deliver it to his house and demand that I put it in his hand to enable me to get decent housing. He lived in Southeast Washington not far from my Mothers' home. I felt like they were going to lock me up making such a demand, so I wanted to leave my children in good hands! I was fired up and mad! I walked up the steps to his door on Alabama Avenue and the security gentleman stationed at the side of the house met me before I reached the Mayors' door. I said, "I want to speak to the Mayor and place this letter in his hand." He said, "Miss, I cannot allow you to place a letter in the Mayor's hand, even if he was here."

In my mind, I never thought about him not being there, I thought I had picked the right time…directly after every ones dinner time. I told the guard my story about my frustration living on Howard Road with my two children, the mice and the roaches and he was very attentive in listening and empathized with me. He assured me that he would give the Mayor my letter, so I placed the letter in his hands.

The next morning, I received a personal call at my job from Mayor Barry himself. He stated he received my letter and gave me the telephone number of the resident manager of a cooperative on Elvans Road, Southeast where the apartments had been recently, completely renovated. I called the resident manager and she was expecting my call because the Mayor had called her before he called me. I went to see the apartment that evening, loved the apartment, filled out an application and she then stated I needed a $500.00 deposit to move in. I asked her to give me two weeks to obtain the $500.00. I thought to myself, "I did not have the money and where was I going to get the $500.00?"

Tuesday morning, as I rushed to the bus stop to get April to school, Phillip to the babysitter and me to work, I met one of Frank's friends on the bus, whom I had not seen in a long time and he asked what was I doing in this area on this side of the bridge. I told him I lived on Howard Road. He said, "What!" He did not know that Frank and I had separated. Later that day, he obviously called Frank and told him that he had seen me because Frank called me that evening to find out specifically where we were living.

To this day, I do not know how Frank obtained my telephone number. I never gave him my telephone number, did not give his friend my telephone number nor was my number listed in the telephone book. I had not communicated with Frank as to where I was moving when we separated.

I invited Frank over that evening to see where we lived because he was concerned. I had a bottle of wine that I had been saving for a special occasion, so when he came over, we drank wine, talked about our children, shared and played with them and put them to bed together. We had a ball that night! (We were separated, but he was still my husband!) When we woke up the next morning, he picked up his glass of wine to take a sip from it and there were at least 32 roaches in the glass whom we figured had also wanted a sip of his wine! He looked at the glass of wine and said, "That's it, You and my babies are getting out of this apartment." I told him about the co-op apartment that I had filled out an application on and that I needed $500.00 to move in it. Within three days, Frank gave me the money to move me and his babies into a newly formed cooperative that had just renovated a 3-bedroom apartment, just for us! We were happy campers! Look how God orchestrated that one!

I remember when.....during another one of my short separations from Frank. We deeply loved one another, but the devil was very busy in our relationship! We had something special, we knew it and everyone around us knew it too, however, the devil was quite mad about it and used every plot and scheme he could to break the bond. He never could break it, only death broke the physical bond!

Moving right along! Phillip was a baby and I was working, but receiving a low salary. I applied for food stamps and got them for six months only because they stated, I worked....this was at the time that the government provided you with paper food stamps that spent like money. I was elated.

This one particular day, I went to the grocery store to purchase food with my food stamps, but I also needed pampers. You cannot buy pampers with food stamps and I had no extra money. I was thinking, "how am I going to get these pampers with no money." Before I arrived at the counter to pay for my food, I wrote a note on a bus transfer that I had decided I was going to give to the cashier. The note stated, "Please let me have these pampers, I do not have the money to pay for them, all I have is food stamps." I said, "Good Morning" to the cashier as it was my turn for her to ring up my purchases and handed the note to her.

She read the note, looked at me and placed the transfer beside her cash register. She started ringing up my food purchases and when she got to the pampers, she pushed the pampers through with the other items. I was so grateful; I thanked that cashier over 20 times before I left the store. Nobody knew, but me, her and God! Who would have thought? It only happened once, but after that, I decided that each month before this six month period is up; I would save $50.00 of my food stamps, so that when the six months was up, I would have stamps left to carry me through. In order to do that, for the last almost week and a half of each of the last three months, my children and I ate canned soup and buttered bread for dinner every night.

Campbell soup was one of my best friends! By the time, my six months was up receiving the food stamps, I had put aside $150.00 worth of food stamps to carry me through, during the rough times when my salary could not stretch. We continued to eat soup the last 1½ weeks of each month…until I got a promotion on my job making more money.

I remember when….My car was in the hospital for a period of time, such a long time when we lived on Howard Road.

I remember when….Many summer evenings after work, Frank and I would take our children to McDonalds, get the carry out and we would go to the Anacostia River and Park in Southeast; lay a blanket out, eat together and the children would play around the big trees as we lounged, cuddled and watched them play.

After they got tired of playing, they would join us on the large blanket and we would all take a nap together. That was over 29 years ago…the Anacostia Park was safer then. I always woke up first and looked around to make sure everything was in tack and would wake Frank up, both of us being so thankful to God that no one hurt us or took anything away from us. God protected us as we all slept like babies near the Anacostia River on those beautiful evenings!

I remember when….I prayed for, hugged and kissed my husband and children everyday!

Many times, I would also anoint my children before sending them off to school.

*I remember when....*Frank and I and our children would <u>always</u> eat together as a family...that is probably why I now do not enjoy eating alone!

*I remember when....*Frank and I decided that we wanted to expose our children to eating in nice restaurants. We took them to one of our favorite restaurants, "The Red Lobster." Phillip was 2 and April was 7. Everything was fine. We settled in a booth and the waitress came over and greeted us and gave us our menus. As Frank and I were looking at the menus....Phillip smiling and excited, hollered out, I have two forks! Frank and I looked at one another and I explained to Phillip that one was for your salad and the other one was for eating the rest of your meal. Frank and I laughed and he said, "We will be taking them out more to restaurants."

*I remember when....*Early one Saturday morning, Phillip drove my car at the age of 16 in the rain, with no license and crashed my car into another car! The person in the car which he hit took my tag number and called their insurance company. After he crashed the car, he drove the car back in the same parking space in front of our home and placed the keys back in my purse as I slept, as if nothing happened.

I woke up that morning, got dressed, fixed breakfast for my children and for Phillip's best friend who had spent the night with us and then went to my car to run some errands. I saw my car and almost had a heart attack.

I could not understand how it happened because my car was at the end of the cul-de-sac and the crashed end was not on the side that a car could hit at the end of our block. I went back into the house and told everyone about my car and Phillip finally admitted that he had drove the car and crashed it. I was dumb-founded…Phillip stated he had been taking my keys while I slept and has been driving for over a year! I told him that he is going to pay for this damage and to get dressed properly, so that I could take him job hunting.

We went to at least 5 businesses in the neighborhood and Phillip begin working his first job that next week in one of the local businesses. He paid off the damage he made to my car. He has now been working since he has been sixteen years old!

*I remember when….*During the summer when I was 17 years old and soon to graduate from the 12th grade at Eastern High School in June, 1969. I decided that I wanted to go to college away from home and my School Counselor had given me a list of colleges that were giving scholarships to honor high school graduates with 3.0 and above grade point averages to come to their colleges. My mother wanted me to stay in Washington, D.C. and go to Howard University. I sent for and received applications from at least 4 out of state colleges, completed the applications, mailed them back and had decided that the first one that gave me a scholarship, I would take it. I was tired of my life being sheltered and controlled by my mother.

I was tired of Saturday being, "clean the house day," wash the clothes, put them on the clothes line, dust and polish <u>all</u> the furniture! I wanted to be free! Hope College in Holland, Michigan sent me a letter accepting me into their college and offered me a one year scholarship with the costs of books included! I ran around our apartment screaming and acting like a crazy woman when I received that letter. Called my mother at work and told her my wonderful news and she congratulated me. For the next week, she walked around depressed and sad about me leaving and I walked around like I had just won the lottery!

That was the year of a remarkable transformation in my life! I did not have to worry about tuition and the costs of my books, but I did have to purchase items to wash my clothes, brush my teeth, make-up, bras, panties, personal items, rollers, hair grease, snacks, etc. I worked two jobs to enable me to purchase those small items which became "big items" when it was now my responsibility to purchase them for myself.

When I lived in my Mothers' house, my mother had always purchased them for me! I worked in the cafeteria serving the students breakfast, lunch and dinner between classes. That job paid a low salary and took care of my snacks. I would take to my room from the cafeteria, the extra packaged snacks that the students did not eat. I know, I became a thief; however, I definitely was not a *hungry* thief! Lord, please forgive me. I had to do what I had to do to survive!

My other job was modeling for the art students in two periods of art classes at $3.00 an hour for two days a week for three hours. This was my good paying job! That job ended when the students asked the teacher to ask me to take off my clothes; they wanted to draw a naked picture of me. I had on a bathing suit this particular day and they wanted me to take it off. I told the teacher, I can pose for the students holding the apples, pears, vases of flowers, as I had done in the past, but not naked. He fired me on the spot from my good paying job, stating that my job was to pose for the students, in whatever poses he or they requested and to fill out my final time sheet to receive my last pay check.

I was upset, yet on the other hand, I left with a feeling of empowerment that I did not understand at that particular time. The students were mad and I was glad! By the time, I walked to my room in the dormitory, I begin to think about the $72.00 per month that I would not be getting and got depressed! I quickly found another job on campus the next week.

I went back home for my first Christmas in 1969, being in college away from home. When I walked in the door, I told my mother, "Ma, the house is so beautiful, the curtains are beautiful, the furniture is beautiful. My mother said, "Louise those are the same curtains at the window and the same furniture that was here when you left and has been in place for years! I came home with a new attitude; I was so appreciate of my home, my mother and the small bedroom that I shared with my sister! Every morsel of food I ate was delicious!

I now looked at the world with different eyes. That was one of the best Christmases I have ever had! When I returned to school, I wrote my sister a letter and told her to listen and do everything Momma tells you to do. I had a new respect and appreciation for the woman who paid the bills and had taken care of me since birth to 17 years of age. In my eyesight....she walked on water and I have always felt that up until the day of her passing!

4

Purpose of Parents

To everyone who thinks that prosperity is only
about cars, houses, jewelry, big salaries and
big pretty homes with your feet sinking in two or
three-inch deep carpet, think again. Prosperity
is molding, training, developing and establishing
your child into fruit as the Word says, that brings
forth fruit.....a fruitful life. Fruit is the result of
developing Christian character. If the goal of the
Christian life may be stated as Christ-likeness,
then surely every trait developed in us should
reflect Christ. His character must be the fruit of
the Spirit. In nine terms in Galatians 5:22-23,
Peter urges the development of seven accompa-
niments to faith in order that we might be fruitful.
In 2 Peter 1:5-8, these terms are common to
both lists: love and self-control. The others are
joy, peace, long-suffering, kindness, goodness,

faithfulness, meekness, virtue, knowledge, endurance, piety, and brotherly love. To show these character traits is to bear fruit in one's life.

Children need to know that their purpose is to serve the Lord Jesus Christ. All children need parents or substitute parents, if they are to grow into fullness and be able to develop all of the potential that is in them. Our job as parents is to recognize the individual potential, talents and gifts that each of our children possess. Cultivate those potentials and make sure they assist in developing every talent and gift that is in them.

Our children are all diamonds, rubies, and jades. They are gifts from God and you must believe it! They are miracles and they are so easy to love. They must be built upon the rock. The rock is Jesus. Families must be committed to Jesus Christ to become and stay strong! J. Richard Fugate in his book entitled, "What the Bible Says About Child Training" says, "Parents must provide strong leadership for their children and stand responsibly for their outside influences. Parents are the symbol and representative of God's authority to their children."

You can have all the material riches in the world, however, if your child is rebellious, negative, in trouble with the police all the time, keeps the family in turmoil and has no respect for himself/herself nor the family, nothing is more distracting than to know that your child is out of control. I heard someone say and I am paraphrasing, "You are as happy as the child in your home, who is the most unhappy."

We live in a world today that has become confused about its morals and values. It is as the Bible speaks in the Scriptures; the world will become richer, but weaker in its values. How do you go about making sure your children prosper? How do you encourage them to be stronger and stay focused? What should you be doing? What is your role? A seed needs water, sunlight, and fertile dirt to grow; our children need love and discipline to grow into mature, caring adults. Love, 1 John 4:19 says, "We love, because he first loved us." Are you amazed at how much God loves us? We must love our children when they are unlovable or do not know how to return love properly. Let us make an assumption here that parent(s) know how to love.

"Beloved, I pray that in all respects you may prosper and be in good health, just as your soul prospers. For I was very glad when brethren came and bore witness to your truth, that is, how you are walking in truth. I have no greater joy than this, to hear of my children walking in the truth." 3 John 1:2-4

The Scripture above was written by John to Gaius who was a convert of John's. Our children are our converts. What do our lives look like? What are we converting them to?

I served and ministered to youth, 16-18 years old at the former Oak Hill Youth Detention

Center in Laurel, Maryland through Greater Mount Calvary Holy Church's Prison Ministry several years ago. Be cognizant of the fact that the powers that are in place, are investing heavily in building jails to hold our children and teenagers. I call them children at Oak Hill because that is exactly what they were. I met a young Black, male teen, 15 years old, whose mother, father, grandmother and aunt were in prison because they all got caught selling drugs. The young man landed in the detention center because he was selling drugs to feed his younger sister and brothers who were left at home. He became the man in the house and did what he saw his relatives do! When he was caught stealing food from a market, his sister and brothers were sent to foster care and he was sent to Oak Hill. An entire family broken down and separated.

I met another young, Black male, 16 years old at Oak Hill expecting his first child. He was so excited! His 15 year old, girlfriend sent him a picture of the baby's' sonogram, (the visual image produced by reflective sound waves). It was an amazing picture... he knew exactly where the particular parts of the body were and pointed them out to me. The picture that became so much clearer to me, was a 15 year old teenager getting prepared to have and raise a baby, and the father was incarcerated. I saw two babies about to attempt to raise another baby. Can it be done? Yes, but much help is needed and it will not be easy! The majority of the weight will fall upon the girl's parents to help raise this child. Fifteen and 16 year olds should be enjoying and exploring their worlds, doing fun activities, moving towards building their careers, thinking about getting their first apartment or house, getting experience working and working towards getting their licenses to get the car of their dreams, which, they cannot yet afford!

You may be thinking to yourself right now, my life does not exemplify the life described above in the Scriptures. Parents, Wake Up! Our children need us. Selling illegal drugs as the "family business" will only lead to destruction of our families. Polly Berends is a veteran childrens' book author who has written several books including, "Whole Child, Whole Parent" and Gently Lead: How To Teach Your Children About God While Finding out for Yourself." She says,

> "Our children need to be comforted, cared for, encouraged, trained, pro-tected, instructed, reprimanded, for-bidden and prevented. But we must also have regard for them, for their right to be wrong or, more correctly, for their ability to learn to be right. Where their mistakes are not dangerous to themselves and do not impinge radi-cally on the rights of others, we must allow them their freedom."

Parents make the difference in children's lives. They will grow up to be who they are because of us or in spite of us. We have the responsibility to train them properly, but we must know what to do.

Matthew 13:24-30, (The New American Standard) states it this way:

"He presented another parable to them, saying, the kingdom of heaven may be compared to a man who sowed good seed in his field. But while men were sleeping, his enemy came and sowed tares also among the wheat, and went away.

But when the wheat sprang up and bore grain, then tares became evident also. And the slaves of the landowner came and said to him, "Sir, did you not sow good seed in your field? How then does it have tares? And he said to them, 'An enemy has done this!' And the slaves said to him, 'Do you want us, then, to go and gather them up?' But he said, "No; lest while you are gathering up the tares, you may root up the wheat with them.

Allow both to grow together until the harvest; and in the time of the harvest I will say to the reapers, "First gather up the tares and bind them in bundles to burn them up; but gather the wheat into my barn."

According to Berends, "the field is each man's consciousness. The seeds are truthful, fruit bearing ideas; the weeds, false hindering ones. We are all the sowers, striving servants sleeping and reapers discerning. The enemy is ignorance passing for knowledge. With regard to our children, as parents, we must simply tend to the wheat. This parable serves as a warning to parents. Parents are laborers; we must produce fruitful lives in our children."

When we tend to the wheat, Isaiah 40:31 becomes real:

"They will mount up with wings like eagles, they will run and not get tired; and they will walk and not become weary."

We must point our children to God. We must teach through revelation and by our example. We must live the Scriptures. We must have standards of conduct and maintenance in the home and it must be insisted that our children abide by those standards. Matthew 5:16 says,

> "Let your light shine before men in such a way that they may see your good works and glorify your Father who is in heaven."

Parents are examples to children. We are on a mission, an assignment. Inconsistent living and unconfessed sin in the lives of parents who are believers will provide a covering which hides the light of God. So we must keep our lives clean before the Lord and before our children. J. Richard Fugate says,

"Raising a child is not training. Plants and animals are raised. To raise something means to grow it. To raise a child would only consist of feeding, clothing, and protecting him from destruction until he reaches physical maturity. While it is true today that most parents are only "raising" their children, raising does not constitute the training of the soul that God intends.

If you desire for your child to become obedient and willing to accept God's standards as his own, you will have to utilize the process that God has designed to obtain these results. Biblical child training produces a quality character much different than would have developed had the child been left alone to grow up according to his own nature. God's Word commands parents specifically to so alter the nature of their children.

Parents must teach God's Word to their children. Deuteronomy 6:6-7 (King James Version), "And these words, which I command thee this day, shall be in thine heart; and thou shalt teach them diligently unto thy children, and shalt talk of them when thou sittest in thine house, and when thou walkest by the way, and when thou liest down, and when thou riseth up."

The Message Bible eloquently states the same scripture above, this way; "Write these commandments that I've given you today on your hearts. Get them inside of you and then get them inside of your children. Talk about them wherever you are, sitting at home or walking in the street; talk about them from the time you get up in the morning to when you fall into bed at night."

Fugate continues to say, "As a parent, you are always training your child, even if you are not teaching him according to God's standards. Simply because you are in the position of ruler ship, your child will receive his direction from you, right or wrong. You set the standards for his acceptable conduct either by what you allow (training by default) or by what you intentionally teach (overt negative training).

If a child is rude, inconsiderate, and selfish, he has been trained to be that way. If a child is lazy and sloppy or is disrespectful and a trouble-maker, he has been trained that way. Parents do not intentionally train their children to reflect these negative characteristics; yet it is very easy because they reinforce his natural inclinations. When parents simply do nothing, the child is trained to think that whatever he wants to do is all right. This inaction is negative training by default.

Parents are training their child when they ignore his negative behavior traits. All parents do this to some extent. We all have blind spots, areas in our own life where we do not see our own faults. These areas tend to block us from training the same problems out of our children. A parent who has poor table manners is unlikely to allow himself to see and correct the atrocious mealtime behavior of his child. A parent who gossips and runs down others is unlikely to recognize and correct this trait. It is difficult to correct negative traits in our children that would condemn ourselves. Parents may teach the principles of right conduct, but if that teaching goes contrary to their own practice, they will not enforce those standards."

We must talk to our children about not taking drugs and to not abuse drinking. It will be difficult to convince your child not to drink when every time you speak of drinking, you have a martini in your hand or they just saw you drink the vodka or the gin with orange juice.

It is difficult to talk to your child about celibacy when you are "shacking" with their father or another man is living in the household. Children are not blind, nor stupid! How can you tell your child not to smoke and you sneak out the front or back door to smoke cigarettes, marijuana and whatever else you can get your hands on.

Bill Cosby says,

"There is no commitment in the world like having children. Even though they often will drive you to consider commitment of another kind, the value of a family still cannot be measured. This commitment, of course, cannot be a part-time thing. The great French writer Andre Malraux said it well: "Without a family, man alone in the world, trembles in the cold."

Fathers are very important in the growth and development of children. This does not mean a fast food father, or a microwave father; one who spends a few minutes in the evenings and those minutes are in punishing, directing or correcting.

But a father who is involved with the child's life from the time he/she is born, feeding, bathing, changing diapers and cuddling. Positive teaching/ training and loving the child is vital.

Joan Barbuto, the author of "The ABC's of Parenting: A Guide To Help Parents and Caretakers Handle Childrearing Problems," says this,

"Good fathers have several basic traits, according to psychiatrist and psychologist. They spend lots of time with their child. Good fathers are home with their children most evenings from the time they are infants and play with them reg- ularly and enjoy them. They also know how to communicate with their children, listen to them, empathize with them, understand their point of view. They don't lecture and criticize. They go to events at their children's school and sometimes take their children to doctor visits, music lessons, little league games, etc.

Good fathers do not discipline their children harshly, they understand they won't always obey, and they treat their children fairly. They earn their children's respect by setting a good example, lis- tening to them, having time for them and loving them. Good fathers raise children who are respon- sible, capable, well-adjusted, and who are likely to be more successful academically than children of absent or uninvolved fathers. Studies have shown that children who have attentive fathers are often half a grade ahead of their classmates in their ability."

Perhaps, you are reading this and you are saying to yourself, I have not been the kind of father that I should have been. My father was not in place to teach me and neither was his father in place for him. I missed much in enjoying and training my children. If your children are still young children, it is not too late to begin to spend more time with them. Educate yourself by reading or taking a parenting course to learn how to be a father. You take time out to learn a trade or hobby, do the same with learning how to be the best parent you can be. If your children are grown, you need to apologize to them and ask for their forgiveness to make it right and start fresh. Step up to the plate and be the kind of father they deserve and need. Your grand-children will offer you another opportunity to get it right!

Provide for their needs and teach them how to provide for their wants at whatever stage they are in their lives. Children will always need their fathers; the _kind_ of need simply changes. At a younger age, they need more hands on, at an older age; they need more advice, direction, coaching and money!

David Reagan, a Christian Bible Scholar, published this in October 12, 2006 and it is still applicable, "Both polls and anecdotal evidence point to the same result: Bible-believing churches are losing their teenagers to the world. Teenagers who grow up in churches are leaving church and going to the world as soon as they get a chance.

One statistic states that only 4% of the teens in evangelical churches stay in church. If that is anywhere close, that is an astounding figure. Churches have drawn the teens with entertainment and fun, but this will not keep them.

Probably, the greatest contributing factor is the home. If the home is not solidly Christian—to the point of serious separation from the world—then the teens will learn their values from the world. We must work harder to exhort parents to be godly parents and then teach them how to do it."

5

Tips for Single Fathers/Mothers

There are more single parents today and we mainly hear and read about single mothers, but there are many single fathers raising children. The US Bureau of the Census, Household and Family Characteristics, March 1998 states: "(1) There are currently 12 million single-parent family groups in the US and 10 million of those are maintained by women. Twenty million of all children in the United States under the age of eighteen live with only one parent. (2) 84% of children who live with one parent live with their mother. (3) Thirty-two percent of all births are to unmarried women (4) the number of single mothers, 9.8 million has remained constant while the number of single fathers grew 25 percent in three years to 2.1 million in 1998. The US Bureau of Children with Single Parents, How they Fare, September, 1997 states, "Of children living with one parent,

- 38% live with a divorced parent
- 35% live with a never-married parent
- 19% live with a separated parent
- 4% live with a widowed parent
- 4% live with a parent whose spouse lives elsewhere because of business or some other reason."

Clearly, single parents are not alone, can it be done? Absolutely, I am a witness and if I did it, so can you! New York Times best selling author, Dr. Kevin Leman, gives six keys to raising happy, healthy children in a single parent home:

"Key 1: Create a plan. Start from where you are now and "take stock of what you do have. It may be a lot more than you think."

Key 2: "Know yourself, Know your child. Before you can figure out what makes your kids tick, you need to know what makes you tick."

Key 3: Gather a team: "Being a lone ranger can get lonely and exhausting, so don't be afraid to ask for help. Other adult role models-especially the opposite sex role models are crucial to the well-being of your child."

Key 4: Focus on the ABC's. "All children long for Acceptance, Belonging and Competence.

Key 5: "Hard questions come up in every home-often at the most embarrassing or inopportune times. Answer only the question your child asks. No more and no less. The best advice I could ever give any parent is: Tell the truth.......in love."

Key 6: Realize it's not about you; it's about the kids.....for now. "Single parenting is a lonely job, with long hours and few breaks for "you time." A good parent is not a "good buddy."

In response to Dr. Leman's Key 6, I must discuss his term "good buddy." The positive characteristics of a "good buddy" are vital for parents to have; listening to your child, being there for your child, sharing with your child. The negative characteristics of a "good buddy" means letting your child have their way at the wrong times and them not feeling your specific consequences for wrong behavior, wrong attitudes and wrong decisions. You cannot allow yourself to be a "good buddy" in the negative fashion! Stay focused on the right circumstances with the right responses in whatever situation comes your way as a parent.

Single mothers can help sons develop a strong sense of themselves as boys; however, mothers *must* arrange male interactions for their sons. Boys are extremely concerned about what a man is, becoming one and how they fit into the world. Single mothers raising boys without positive male role models in their lives will develop and grow up sons, whose insecurities will make it common for them to drop out of peer relationships in their teen years and many times lose their "sexual identity." I remember a friend of mine who was concerned that his baby's mama wore skimpy lingerie all the time around their son. Young male children are impressionable and he noticed his son at the age of 8, liking frilly clothes, soft, lacey clothing and he spoke to his sons' mother about "changing up" in how she dresses around their son. She changed her presentation of herself around their son which alleviated a problem that could have become quite serious.

"Look for serious and positive male role models in less obvious places. Encourage your sons' friendships with boys who have a father and brothers who are positive. Allow your boys to spend plenty of time with them. Whenever you have the choice, choose male teachers. Look into Big Brothers, sports, coaching and other mentoring programs, but be mindful that you choose a reputable organization, one that completes background checks on their employees.

It really helps a son feel relaxed and comfortable with you and with him if you learn about the hobbies and activities that interest him. Go to his games and watch him play." Personally, I went to all of my son's games, rallied and hollered to encourage him when he played basketball as if he were "Michael Jordan." I many times called him "Jordan" while he was playing. I also attended all of my daughters' tap dance and jazz recitals and applauded as if she was a female, "Gregory Hines" or a clone of Mable Lee, a well known tap dancer from Atlanta, Georgia. I must admit, I was always publicly, a very "loud and proud mother" when it came to cheerleading for my children. When they were younger, they were embarrassed by it…when they got older, they felt proud and stuck out their chest. I cheer leaded the majority of the time, especially after Frank passed…all by myself! I remember when my daughter, April was graduating from middle school in Albuquerque, New Mexico and got in a fight with another girl one week before graduation!

She was suspended for a week and I was devastated because April was an honor roll student and was about to miss her graduation. Three days before graduation, the Principal called me and stated, "We normally do not make exceptions, inviting students back for graduation if they are on suspension, but April has attained the highest academic award that a student can receive, she has received The Presidential Award and we have to present the award to her at graduation!" I was the happiest mother on earth that day. The day of the graduation, they told parents, beforehand, that everyone should save their applause until the end of the ceremony. We complied, until they called April's name and presented her with The Presidential Award. After she got it in her hand and the Administrators took pictures……I lost it. I stood up and said, "That's my Baby, Hallelujah… the highest award anyone can receive. My baby is the smartest person in this school, Hallelujah!

Hallelujah! Hallelujah!" No one told me to sit down, so I finally got tired of shouting and sat down! The ceremony was never quite the same after I finished, because all the other parents began to cheer-lead each of their children. The school officials intervened one more time and asked parents to be quiet. Soon, they settled in and saw that it was a useless task to keep us quiet; they let us have our way and celebrate our children... *Our Way*! That was one of my most memorable graduations for my daughter!

Mothers, teach not only your daughters, but also teach your sons how to wash dishes, cook, clean the house, mop the floor, iron clothes, keep his room neat and pick up after himself. One day, he will be on his own and there may not be another to pick up after him and do for him. Consider the fact that some men are sloppy because their mother did everything for them. Choose not to raise a sloppy, untidy boy who will grow up to become a sloppy, untidy man!

"Single Moms: When your girlfriends are around you and your son, make sure you and all of the girls avoid "talking down" about males. Before your son reaches the adolescent stage, find ways to talk to him about how their bodies will be changing. Talk matter-of-fact about how and when their bodies will change, but be serious as well. Just know that, as sons mature, there is a temptation to become flirtatious with them. Laughter in each other's presence is always a plus; flirting, however, pushes past the limit of parent/child boundaries.

In the earlier years of a child's life, the job of single fathers raising a daughter is eased by the many women in children's lives, the day-care providers and teachers, as well as women in their extended families.

This is good, but fathers also need to be aware. Like mothers raising sons, you too, have to go out of your way to discover with your daughter and share in her interests and hobbies. As you work to allow your daughter her femininity, don't fall into the trap of stereotyping, assigning her certain chores because society has viewed them as "women's work." Teach her how to check the oil and transmission fluid in your car, put gas in the car, put air in the tires, handle a fire extinguisher and how to mow a lawn. Don't try to turn your daughter into your maid.

As she approaches pre-adolescence, you have important responsibilities facing you. Seek reliable and complete information about how and when females mature physically, and be prepared to address your own daughter's maturation sooner than you may think. Be aware of how you may react to your daughter's new physical maturity. Many fathers, including those who were close to their daughters before adolescence, become uncomfortable about how to treat their daughters as they develop physically. A result of this dilemma causes fathers to withdraw emotionally and physically from their daughters. The result is a daughter who is abruptly cut off from her dad and without a clue as to why. Father, don't cut yourself off. Be honest; share your dilemma with your daughter. She is becoming a woman and this will call for a change in the way you treat one another physically. Hugs and kisses are always wonderful. If you find yourself physically stimulated by any interaction, no matter how innocent, it is time to remember those boundaries.

Be sure your daughter understands that any change in your behavior toward her has everything to do with her maturing and is not a form of punishment or withdrawal on your part. Reassure her that the love and emotional closeness between the two of you "remains solid."

Throughout this book, you will read that children are a blessing! Do you realize that the prosperity of our children is greatly depended on our obedience as parents to God? Psalm 128:13, (New American Standard Version) eloquently states it this way,

"How blessed is everyone who fears the Lord, who walks in His ways. When you shall eat of the fruit of your hands, you will be happy and it will be well with you. Your wife shall be like a fruitful vine, within your house, your children like olive plants around your table."

Stephen R. Covey in his book entitled, "The 7 Habits of Highly Effective Families says, *"You cannot not model. It's impossible."* "People will see your example-positive or negative--as a pattern for the way life is to be lived. As one unknown author so beautifully expressed it:

"If a child lives with criticism, he learns to condemn.

If a child lives with security, he learns to have faith in himself.

If a child lives with hostility, he learns to fight.

If a child lives with acceptance, he learns to love.

If a child lives with fear, he learns to be apprehensive.

If a child lives with recognition, he learns to have a goal.

If a child lives with pity, he learns to be sorry for himself.

If a child lives with approval, he learns to like himself.

If a child lives with jealousy, he learns to feel guilty.

If a child lives with friendliness, he learns that the world is a nice place in which to live."

6

What…The Book of Proverbs?

The Book of Proverbs was important to me in raising my children when they were young as water is to a fish to survive. The Proverbs encouraged, strengthened and gave me stamina and rejuvenation. I read Proverbs everyday…it may have only been 5-10 minutes in the morning, but after reading, it gave me the refreshing that a 10 minute "power nap" gives you. So what is the big deal about the Book of Proverbs? Eugene H. Peterson eloquently voices an introduction in his Message Bible to the Book of Proverbs this way, "Many people think that what's written in the Bible has mostly to do with getting people into heaven— getting right with God, saving their eternal souls. It does have to do with that, of course, but not mostly. It is equally concerned with living on this earth---living well, living in robust sanity. In our Scriptures, heaven is not the primary concern, to which earth is a tagalong after thought. 'On earth as it is in heaven' is Jesus' prayer. 'Wisdom' is the biblical term for this on-earth-as-it-is in heaven everyday living. Wisdom is the art of living skillfully in whatever actual conditions we find ourselves. It has virtually nothing to do with information as such, with knowledge as such. A college degree is no certification of wisdom---nor is it primarily concerned with keeping us out of moral mud puddles, although it does have a profound moral effect upon us. Wisdom has to do with becoming skillful in honoring our parents and raising our children, handling our money and conducting our sexual lives, going to work and exercising leadership, using words well and treating friends kindly, eating and drinking healthily, cultivating emotions within ourselves and attitudes toward others that make for peace. Threaded through all these items is the insistence that the way we think of and respond to God is the most practical thing we do. In matters of everyday practicality, nothing, absolutely nothing, takes precedence over God. Proverbs concentrates on these concerns more than any other book in the Bible. Attention to the here and now is everywhere present in the stories and legislation, the prayers and the sermons, that are spread over the thousands of pages of the Bible. Proverbs distills it all into riveting images and aphorisms that keep us connected in holy obedience to the ordinary."

After putting my children to bed, I would lie on my couch, relax and be still and say, "God talk to me." And He would. Those were my most intimate times. I received direction and wisdom through reading Proverbs and listening to God. You must spend quiet time alone with God, He is real! Some of my favorite proverbs for parents taken from the New International Version of the Bible from the following website, www.upamerica. org are as follows:

10:1 "The Proverbs of Solomon: A wise son brings joy to his father, but a foolish son grief to his mother.

12:1 Whoever loves discipline loves knowledge, but he who hates correction is stupid.

13:1 A wise son heeds his father's instruction, but a mocker does not listen to rebuke.

13:18 He who ignores discipline comes to poverty and shame, but whoever heeds correction is honored.

13:24 He who spares the rod hates his son, but he who loves him is careful to discipline him.

15:5 A fool spurns his father's discipline, but whoever heeds correction shows prudence.

15:10 Stern discipline awaits him who leaves the path; he who hates correction will die.

15:20 A wise son brings joy to his father, but a foolish man despises his mother.

17:6 Childrens' children are a crown to the aged, and parents are the pride of their children.

17:21 To have a fool for a son brings grief; there is no joy for the father of a fool.

17:25 A foolish son brings grief to his father and bitterness to the one who bore him.

19:13 A foolish son is his father's ruin, and a quarrelsome wife is like a constant dripping.

19:18 Discipline your son, for in that there is hope; do not be a willing party to his death.

19:26 He who robs his father and drives out his mother is a son who brings shame and disgrace.

19:27 Stop listening to instruction, my son, and you will stray from the words of knowledge.

22:6 Train a child in the way he should go, and when he is old, he will not turn from it.

22:15 Folly is bound up in the heart of a child, but the rod of discipline will drive it far from him.

23:13 Do not withhold discipline from a child; if you punish him with the rod, he will not die.

23:14 Punish him with the rod and save his soul from death.

29:15 The rod of correction imparts wisdom, but a child left to himself disgraces his mother.

29:17 Discipline your son, and he will give you peace; he will bring delight to your soul."

7

Where Are The Fathers?

athers are important in the lives of children. I
never had the opportunity to meet my father
until I was twenty-two years old and he was in his
coffin. Yes, the very first time I met my father was
at his home going service! Never had a conversation nor the opportunity to ask him any "Why"
questions that may have resolved some of my
own "father issues." I could only take those issues
to God and discuss with my mother and husband
to be, at that time. Traumatic, but better late than
never, I did get the opportunity to meet him! The
benefits that came out of that meeting was having
the opportunity to meet my fathers' family which
included my grandmother on my fathers' side
whom I was named after. My mothers' mother
was also named "Louise" so I had no choice as
to what they were going to name me! I became

very close to my aunt, my fathers' sister and also met my other siblings through the union of my fathers' only marriage which, of course, was not to my mother.

I realize now, but not at that particular time, my husband, Frank use to say to me often, "Louise, you married me because you saw your father in me." Reflecting back on his words, I think there was much truth to those statements to me. Frank was older and I was drawn to him because he imparted wisdom, took the time to cultivate me, and supported me in reaching my dreams/goals, emotionally, spiritually and financially. We were supportive of each other and were each other's cheerleader and best friend! God orchestrated our union. My husband was a natural romantic; he brought me flowers, took me out to dinner, cooked delicious meals *especially* for me, took me to movies, plays and concerts; bought me clothes and many times had them laid out on our bed as a surprise for me when I came home. He <u>knew</u> my size of clothing and lingerie and he was always very attentive. So was I! Frank would spontaneously plan trips and tell me to go pack our bags and let's go and he meant it! I always had our clothes cleaned and luggage ready to go at all times and loved to be spontaneous and get up and GO! He has definitely been a hard act to follow. I have loved and been loved and know how it is supposed to go! One of my former pursuers, several years ago stated to me, after me telling him about Frank, "I am competing with a dead man!" I have been blessed and favored because it could have been quite different in my life growing up without a father in my life. I have had wonderful, positive and encouraging uncles, male teachers and male cousins as my models growing up.

Fathers' input and roles are vital to the welfare and well-being of children growing into healthy adults. God made it that way, fathers and mothers, together raising their children, preparing them to make an impact on the world!

Many Black, male fathers are separated from their children and are not in place in the homes because they are either imprisoned, on the streets selling or on drugs, in homeless shelters, or in mental institutions. Others have re-married and are currently taking care of somebody else's children or have moved on with their lives because of chaos in the relationship with their childrens' mother. Some call it "baby mama drama!" It is not always the babys' mama who has the issues. If men and women knew their roles and purpose and lived out their roles the way God intended, there would be no "baby mama" or "baby daddy drama." The following excerpts taken from the late Dr. Myles Monroe, eloquently explains the role of fatherhood in his book entitled, "The Principles of Fatherhood."

"The highest honor God can give a man is to designate him a father. That does not mean he is bigger or stronger than the female. "Father" is the title or designation God chose for Himself. God does not call Himself "Mother." So if God chooses "Father" as His own title and conveys it upon the man, then it must be the highest title, designation, and honor that any human being can have. In fact, fatherhood is the ultimate work of the male man. Fatherhood is a heavy honor and a tremendous responsibility. A male can do nothing greater than fathering. He can earn a million dollars, but if he fails to fulfill God's calling upon him to father as *God fathers*, then he is a failure. He can own a huge home; have tremendous real estate holdings, manage a large stock portfolio, and have a billion-dollar estate, but if he fails to father his family and children, he is a failure.

A man who is physically strong, but weak as a father is not a man. A man rich in possessions, but poor in fathering is not a man. A man eloquent in Words, but silent as a father in teaching his household the Word and precepts of God is not a father. The measure of a man's success is directly related to his effectiveness as a godly father, for which God is the only true example and standard.

At the root of sin is the absence of real fathers in our world. The sin problem is a fatherhood problem, because sin is the result of a man--Adam--who declared independence from God, his Source and Father. Adam believed he didn't need a father and that he could be a father without the Father. That is when the human race fell into rebellion against God. One of the root meanings of the word sin, armatia, is separation. Adam separated himself from his Father and fell into a state of separation and sin. In other words, man could be called a "fatherless child" because of his own choice. Imagine that. Orphaned by choice! Homeless by choice! Separated from his Father by choice! How tragic was the choice of Adam to reject his Father!

Salvation is the result of a man—Jesus, the Second Adam—providing us with the way to return to the Father. When the Second Adam, Jesus, came to earth, He returned the orphaned children of humanity back to their Father, God. Remember, Adam left his Father. The mission of Jesus was to return humanity—fatherless, orphaned humanity— back to the Father. Malachi prophesied that this would happen when John the Baptist prepared the way for the Messiah:

> '*He will turn the hearts of the fathers*
> *to their children, and the hearts of*
> *the children to their fathers; or else*
> *I will come and strike the land with a*
> *curse.' (Malachi 4:6)*

Adam was a fatherless child, and Adam had children. The first child that came out of Adam was a female—Eve. Adam's first baby was not

Cain; Adam's first baby was a woman named Eve. Every child after Eve was fatherless because there was no God-father. Since Adam was fatherless, all of his descendants were also fatherless, starting with Eve.

God breathed life into Adam. *"The LORD God formed the man from the dust of the ground and breathed into his nostrils the breath of life, and the man became a living being." (Genesis 2:7)*

But Adam cut himself off from God, his Father—the Source of his creation and life. Once Adam became fatherless, all he could pass onto his children was death. The father can only create or generate in his children what he has received from his father. Father is the source, the creator, the generator and the progenitor. Future generations can receive only what the father gives them.

Since Adam rejected his Father, thereby rendering him fatherless, the only inheritance he had to give to future generations was sin and death—a fatherless inheritance. As a fatherless child, Adam's bequest to humanity was fatherlessness.

One more point needs to be made here. If Adam's first child was a woman, and Adam was fatherless, then all women, starting with Eve, are fatherless. That means women are looking for just one thing—a father, not a husband. They are suffering from fatherlessness. All too often, women are lost and making so many mistakes because all they have in the house is a husband, not a father. What they need is a father who can teach them about the Father, God. Without fathers, there is a curse upon women and future generations. In essence, every husband must also become his wife's father. This is a curse that still affects us today!"

In summary, fathers, be there for your children. Husbands, be there for your wives. Be in place for your family! Pray for your children's minds, that they would seek wisdom, Godly advice and understanding. That they would appreciate and value knowledge and discernment and that their thoughts would stay centered on the truth of God's Word. With all the social media and high tech gadgets, ask God to guard your children's eyes and protect their innocence. Pray that they would focus their attention on *choosing* to make the right decisions.

Ask God to give your children an open, cheerful and happy heart! Pray that your children would come to know the Lord early and would place their trust totally in Him. Pray that your children would be diligent and focused in their work and that their hands would not be idle, and that God would bless and establish the work of their hands. Pray that your children would be quick to hear and listen to instructions. Ask God to protect and direct your children's tongues from evil and their lips from speaking lies and that the words that come out of their mouths would be pleasing to God and strength and inspiration to others. Everyday, pray Psalm 1:1 over your children's lives and personalize this scripture by specifically adding your child's name in the scripture, "Blessed is the one who does not walk in step with the wicked or stand in the way that sinners take or sit in the company of mockers." Always ask God to order and direct your children's steps and decisions.

8

Cut Out The Cursing!

❦

S ome parents talk better to their cats and dogs than to their own children. It is quite disturbing to hear mothers and fathers in the grocery store, at the bus stops and on trains, loudly cursing at their children to ask them to do minor tasks. Simply saying sit down does not require you to call out the part of their body that they will sit down with…by calling it the other name used for a donkey. It is unacceptable.

It is obvious that the children are used to it because when I look into their faces, they are usually, _not_ embarrassed. I am embarrassed for them because I know they hear worse "curse words" than that at home! I was never a cussing mother. I heard my mother "curse," but never at or to me. I never cursed at or to my children when they were younger. NEVER! My children have never heard me curse until they both were grown! I don't know what happened to me, but on this one particular day, not too long ago, when I turned 60, I think I just felt grown enough to say anything I wanted to say and it was the word, "damn" which was a response to something both of them said, "they bust out laughing when they heard me say it. They said, "Ma, when did you start cursing?" Truthfully, I never knew how to curse, because it was never a part of who I am.

Parents: cursing just simply means you have not mastered the English language. You are teaching your children to curse when they get frustrated and teaching them that it is normal to intentionally plant a few curse words throughout their conversation. Stop cursing your children out! It is unbecoming, unchristian and ungodly!

9

Being A Step-Parent

B lended families are quite common. Let's get married and you bring your children and I will bring mine to the marriage! I read a very interesting article that gave excellent tips and advice on this subject entitled, "9 Step Parenting Do's and Don'ts" by Colleen Oakley at this website address below. I have listed them below the website address: http://www.webmd.com/parenting/features/tips-for-stepparents

1. DON'T come on too strong.

"Many stepparents try too hard to create an instant bond," says Christina Steinorth, MFT, author of *Cue Cards for Life: Gentle Reminders for Better Relationships*. "Though they have good intentions, many stepparents try to buy their stepchild's love through lots of gifts or by being the really cool parent. Kids can see right through that." Be realistic -- and be yourself. You'll have a better chance of developing that close relationship you long for.

2. DO get on the same parenting page with your new spouse -- and his or her ex.

"All the parents need to discuss their methods -- rewards, punishments, chores, allowances, bedtimes, homework -- and come to an agreement about the rules," says Tina B. Tessina, PhD, author of *Money, Sex and Kids: Stop Fighting about the Three Things That Can Ruin Your Marriage.* "The transition is much easier if the parents are in accord. If something happens you haven't discussed, just defer to one parent, and work it out later."

3. DO encourage your stepchild to have one-on-one time with both of his or her biological parents.

"Some stepparents are threatened by their stepchildren spending time alone with their biological parent -- especially their spouse's ex -- but they shouldn't be," Steinorth says. "When you're supportive of it, you're sending the message that this isn't a competition for affection and that you truly want to see your stepchildren happy."

4. DO have family meetings weekly.

Give everyone, including the kids, a chance to share how they feel, what they like and don't like, and ask them to share both positive and negative opinions," Tessina says. "Ask for suggestions about how to make things better."

5. DON'T set your expectations too high.

"This is especially important for stepparents that already have children of their own," Steinorth says. "You may feel that you'll be able to step into a new family and have the same interactions, feelings, and bonds you share with your biological children. What new stepparents seem to forget is that they have a shared history with their biological children that they don't have with their stepchildren. Give your 'new family' time to develop its own unique dynamic, without any pressure of how you think it should be."

6. DON'T overstep your bounds.

"A big mistake many stepparents make is over-disciplining a child in an attempt to gain respect," Barrow says. "This often backfires and causes the kid to despise them. I recommend stepping back and allowing the primary parent to discipline their own children for at least the first year. After you've spent time earning their affection and respect, then you have a much better chance of being listened to."

7. Be ready to hear, "You're not my real mom/dad."

"This is a stepchild's way of trying to take power away from your role," Steinorth says. Be ready with an appropriate response.

"When it happens, the key is to not deny what your stepchild is telling you. Keep it factual and avoid the power struggle." Your best bet? "You're right, I'm not your biological parent, I'm your stepparent. But that doesn't mean I love or care about you less."

8. DO plan activities with your stepchild.

Bike together, go bowling, take an art class together, or even go grocery shopping and cook dinner together once or twice a week. "Shared experiences are a great way to bond with stepchildren," Steinorth says. "Try to carve out one-on-one time together at least once a month."

9. DON'T take it personally.

"Just remember that your stepchildren are dealing with their own feelings about the end of their biological parents' marriage," Steinorth says.

When parent's divorce, many children still hold out hope that their parents will work things out and get back together. But when a stepparent comes into the picture, the new stepparent is, in essence, putting an end to that dream. Kids mourn the loss of what they had hoped could be, and those feelings take time to work through."

Ron Deal in a Focus on the Family article speaks eloquently about "Smart Step Parenting" in the following website: http://www.focusonthefamily.com/parenting/parenting-roles/blended-families/smart-stepparenting

"Parenting in stepfamilies is a two, three, or four-person (sometimes more!) dance. Parent-stepparent harmony is the crux of successful parenting within your home. The two most critical relationships in any stepfamily home are the marriage and the stepparent-stepchildren relationships.

The marriage must be strong to endure the many pressures that stepfamily couples face and provide the backbone to stepfamily stability. Almost as important is the stepparent-stepchildren relationship. The stepparent's role in the family is critical because it dramatically affects the level of stress in children. Less stress in children equals more harmony with stepparents; that in turn leads to more harmony in the marriage.

Many people assume incorrectly that step parenting is the sole responsibility of the stepparent. This assumption pits husband and wife against one another when the stepparent flounders or upsets the children. On the contrary, step parenting is a two-person task.

Biological parents and stepparents must work out roles that complement one another and play to each other's strengths. Just as in two-biological parent homes, parents and stepparents must be unified in goals and work together as a team. Stepparents who are struggling need biological parents who will step up to the plate.

Stepparents and biological parents do not function in a vacuum, isolated from one another. In fact, what is needed most is a working alliance between the parent and stepparent that helps to clarify the stepparent's role. Smart step parenting means planning and parenting together."

10

Golden Nuggets ~ Author To Parents

Everyone's schedule is different. Therefore, it is difficult to sit at the table to eat meals together daily with the entire family. Do it every evening that you can; summer time, holidays, and during school. Eat breakfast together every Sunday before or after church depending on the early or late service you attend discussing the service or other topics. Make dinners and breakfast special, not only the food, but the conversation; share positive things and thoughts. Frank loved to cook fish, steak, fried potatoes and onions, and big pancakes the size of the frying pan....I miss that man!

At the dinner table, share good conversation! Adults/parents, bring only positive teaching, correcting, encouraging, and strengthening comments to the table. Be as loving and kind as you can at those meals. Share one good thing you love about each other! Take this opportunity to tell your children good things about themselves. Start TODAY, they will remember these times when they are adults!

I remember several years ago, I invited my former Pastor, his wife and children for dinner in my small apartment. I asked him to say the grace and we all held hands. We closed our eyes and held hands at least three-four minutes before he began to pray.....so I opened my eyes as did everyone else to find out why it was taking him so long to begin to pray, (we were hungry). He was softly crying....big tears rolling down his eyes. Everyone was surprised and we then asked him, "What was wrong?" He finally said, he could not remember the last time he sat down with his entire family together and had dinner. It touched him and he told us so! We had a wonderful dinner after he prayed and I do not think dinner at his home was ever the same!

- Give your children compliments the same way you point out faults, mistakes, etc. Always remember, you are teaching them how to handle their future families and relationships. Praise them in public, criticize them privately.

- When was the last time you sang to your children, *I love you...just thinking about my children (I place their name in the song to make it personal)....blows my mind.* You make it personal by placing their name in the song! I used to sing those lines above to my children all the time.......to this day....I still sing those lyrics to them and they now sometimes call me and sing the lyrics to me or text them to me!

- Decide to show more love to your children. Take them on dates doing the things THEY love to do, individually and together. I took my children on individual dates and it was their special time to go where they wanted to go; to a movie, skating, the playground or out to eat.

- Do more as a family...remember you are building memories...there are so many free activities available in the DC metropolitan area. Take the free boat ride up the Potomac River offered by the Bladensburg Water Park located on Landover Road in Landover, Maryland on Saturdays and Sundays during the summer. Find the free boat ride offered up the river in your specific state! Google it!

- Enroll the entire family in a class together at the Sports and Learning Complex Center, 8001 Sheriff Road in Landover, Maryland and let the children choose the course. They learn how to parent a family by how you parent them. Find your Sports and Learning Complex that offers swimming, dancing, budgeting, gymnastics and a variety of other courses in the specific state that you live!

- Hug your children everyday.......give them real, wholehearted, meaningful, hugs!

- Pray EVERYDAY together as a family and take your needs to God! Pray for your children's needs, wants and desires and yours too. START THIS NOW!

- Fill your child's emotional tank everyday by telling them the following when the situation deems appropriate:

    1. I Love You!
    2. I am Proud of You!
    3. Always Do Your Best!
    4. Do You Need Help?
    5. You Made a Very Good Decision!
    6. Great Job!
    7. Congratulations!
    8. Way To Go!

9. I Thank God for You!
10. What Would I do Without You?

- Learn how to say "I'm sorry" or "I apologize" to your children when you make a mistake or say something hurtful.

- Don't curse your children out; unless you want them to eventually curse you out. Remember you are teaching them how! Those parents who curse at their children on a regular basis are probably saying, "I wish they would curse me out! They won't have any teeth." Do as I say and not as I do is unacceptable in this case. God gave you children to be a model for them to live and grow stronger. Be a model!

Children can and will get on your last nerve at times. You must always remember that you are a model for them; lazy people, out of habit continually curse because they have not learned to put the English language together to make it work. They curse out of anger and frustration.

There is a way to say everything to honestly get the attention and touch the hearts of your toddlers, children, and grown children. Share your feelings. Share what is in your heart and make it plain, don't take the lazy way out by cursing! For some children, getting cursed out all the time is normal for them. Could it be that, that is the reason these children become the kind of adults where every third word they say is a curse word? Parents, you harvest what you plant!

- One of the most beautiful places in Washington, D. C. and it is a well-kept secret is: the National Arboretum in Northeast Washington, D. C. I used to take my children and I now take my grand-children. We especially enjoyed the duck pond where they had the fattest fish I have ever seen. No fishing is allowed, but, it is a breath-taking, peaceful place. It makes you feel as if you are in another world and it is free!

- In my experience, God seems to bless the child that parents reject or whom the parent has not deposited in one child as much as they have another child. Be mindful to treat all of your children with respect and take care of their individual needs; do not allow favoritism to destroy your relationships.

- Many parents think that when a child reaches eighteen, they need to be on their own, they are grown. Yes, society says they are grown at 18, but are they really? Is your child totally prepared for the responsibilities of their own residence? Are their work ethics and money management skills in place to handle life outside of your home? How did they handle work ethics and money management while residing in your home? That is an indication of whether they are ready or not. Stop putting *unprepared* children out of your house because they are 18? I left home when I was 22 and I left with a generous savings account which I saved, a car, my new china, silverware, pots and pans that I had never used and had bought and stored under my bed for over a year, to be used when I was ready to move! I was prepared to move. Parents; assist in preparing your children to do the same!

- Many times men do not treasure the DNA of a child that is not his own. Many times women do not treasure the DNA of a child that is not her own. Wake up young and single parents who are dating. Your children are priority and come first! Shelter them, always keep the lines of communication open and talk to your children and listen to what they have to say... about everything.

11

An Inheritance For Your Children

The Bible says in Proverbs 13:22, "A good man leaves an inheritance for his children's children, but a sinner's wealth is stored up for the righteous."

I intend to do what the Bible says! When many families lose the breadwinner, the Patriarch or the Matriarch, many members have to start all over again. Many times, nothing is left, but unpaid bills. It is a horrific pattern of a curse. I have decided to do as the Bible states and leave a legacy. Put life insurance in place; let your children know where the policies are located. You may be a parent who worries about what your wealth will do to your children, you are not alone. I have told my children what I am going to leave them and have told them, please do not sell my investments off to simply pay your bills, I have worked too hard to accumulate what I have! My initial concern was that they were ill-equipped to handle my investments if I suddenly died, so I am trying to teach them to handle my business/investments. I sometimes worry that by providing too much money will rob my children of the ambition and hard work that it took for me to amass the wealth, but both of them are hard-workers and self-sufficient, pay their own bills and handle their own financial affairs which is truly a blessing for me! I am grateful! So they do have some understanding!

My children are currently in their 30's. I tested them, unbeknownst to them, I gave them each a nice piece of money with no restrictions and sat back and watched to see what they did with the money because my thinking was; how they handle this small amount will tell me how they will handle a large amount. They did not take a trip to Atlantic City or New York. Both paid off some of their debts, son brought equipment for his business, and both took care of family health needs in their individual families. They did not blow the money! I am looking in them for a pattern of making good financial decisions and looking for improvement.

The legacy I am building must be protected from my children themselves, creditors, lawsuits and other people in their lives who may try to take advantage of them. It is obvious to me that they have made plans for their futures. I have asked them both to take courses in personal finances to enable them to enjoy, manage, _keep_ and _continue_ to build on an inheritance when they receive it. I will continue to build a legacy for my children and grand-children.

Most importantly, build a legacy of faith in your children! Pastor Creflo Dollar eloquently wrote an article entitled, "Giving Your Children an Inheritance of Faith, Part 2" and it reads as follows:

"The New Testament tells us about one particular young man who received an inheritance of faith. His name was Timothy, and he pastored some of the great early churches that were started by the Apostle Paul.

In 2 Timothy 1:3-5, Paul wrote to him and said, "...Without ceasing I have remembrance of thee in my prayers night and day; Greatly desiring to see thee, being mindful of thy tears, that I may be filled with joy; When I call to remembrance the unfeigned faith that is in thee, which dwelt first in thy grandmother Lois, and thy mother Eunice; and I am persuaded that in thee also."

Timothy was in a bad situation when Paul wrote to him—but he made it through in victory, mainly because he had an inheritance of faith!

Teaching the Principles

Sadly enough, many Christian parents today aren't giving their children what Timothy's relatives provided for him. They aren't handing down their faith. The reason is simple. They just don't know how.

I can't tell you everything you need to know about passing down your faith to your children, but I can tell you a few simple truths that will get you started, truths that have helped me greatly in recent years.

The first one is so obvious; it seems we should hardly need to say it. Yet, most of us have to admit we haven't fully incorporated it into our lives. It is this: We must take the time not just to learn the principles of the Word ourselves, but also to teach them to our children.

Deuteronomy 6:5-7 says it this way: "Thou shalt love the Lord thy God with all thine heart, and with all thy soul, and with all thy might. And these words, which I command thee this day, shall be in thine heart: And thou shalt teach them diligently unto thy children, and shalt talk of them when thou sittest in thine house, and when thou walkest by the way, and when thou liest down, and when thou risest up."

Notice verse 6 says the Word must be in your heart—not in your head, in your heart! You are not going to be able to impart into the lives of your children a truth you just mentally agree is true. You must have that Word living and established inside you. You must have revelation knowledge of how it works. You must have applied it and seen it produce results in your own life. Then, and only then, will you be able to explain that Word to your children in a meaningful way.

Also, notice that verse says you should talk about the Word when you sit in your house. That means this is not just a Sunday ritual. You need to sit down at home and talk to your child in a practical way about the Word.

You don't have to get deep and theological about it. (Please don't!) Leave off the "thees" and "thous." Just show your child how the Word applies to him and his world.

Take advantage of the opportunities that arise when you're sitting around the table. Learn how to weave the Word of God into every conversation. For example, when your son starts telling you about all the girls he's interested in, that's an excellent opportunity to do some weaving.

You might say, "You know son, the reason we like girls so much is because God made men that way. In the very beginning, He looked at Adam and said, 'Boy, you don't need to be alone!' Then He put him to sleep, took out one of his ribs, and made a wife for him.

"My goodness, she was a masterpiece. He made her so wonderfully that when Adam woke up and saw her, he said, 'Wow! I feel good!' We still feel that way today, don't we, son? But one thing you need to remember: God just took one rib and made one woman for Adam. There weren't any spare ribs lying around, and there weren't any spare women. I want you to understand that you're destined to find that one woman God made for you...."

What have you imparted to your son through a conversation like that? You've taken away the worldly principle that says, "Fool around with as many women as you can," and replaced it with God's principle of marriage and faithfulness to one person. That's the way to teach the Word.

Give Them a Pattern...and Be Persistent

The second thing you must do if you want to plant good seed in the heart of your child and leave them with an inheritance of faith is this: Give them a pattern. Let your life be a living example of how faith works.

Children learn more by watching what we do than by listening to what we say. You can talk the Christian talk, but if you come home and complain about your day at work, if you blame the boss and the secretary for all your problems and act like none of them are your fault, that's what your child will learn to do. Before you know it, he'll be coming home from school blaming his teacher and his classmates for situations instead of accepting responsibility himself.

By the same token, what if you run into a difficult time at work, and you've been told you're going to be laid off? If you come home and say, "Come on, kids, let's pray—the company is cutting my job, but the Word of God says blessing and increase are mine. So let's pray and believe God is in control of our circumstances." Your children are going to learn not to panic, but to pray and trust God.

The third thing you must do to train your children in the ways of God is to be persistent. They must see you hang in there and do what needs to be done—when it is convenient and when it isn't. There are times in all our lives when we say to ourselves, "I wish I could just break down and cry. I wish I could just forget this faith business for a few minutes and speak doubt and unbelief." But when you're tempted to do that, remember your children are watching you. They are waiting to see how you are going to respond to this situation so they'll know how to respond when it happens to them.

So get yourself together, and be persistent in your faith!

Participate, Give Positive Praise and Pray

The fourth important element that's necessary if you want to impart faith to your children is participation. Something positive happens when you get involved in what concerns or interests them. Through participation, you can establish a caring relationship that makes it easier for you to communicate with them and teach them the values and life skills they need to know. When your son comes home from school with a problem, do you think, "Here's an opportunity to participate," or do you say, "I don't have time to mess with this, son! You handle it yourself!"

Of course, you might never say such a thing out loud - but you may well be saying it very clearly with your actions. If you don't find the time to attend your child's band concerts and school plays, if you don't take the time to talk with your child about that problem at school, to pray with him about it and visit his teacher if necessary, the message you're communicating is this—I don't care. And that is one message that children never forget.

The fifth tool you can use to train up your child in the way he or she should go is positive praise. It's the greatest motivation for doing what's right. We always seem to have time to tell children what they've done wrong. But how often do we take the time to tell them what they've done right? If you don't do that very often, make a conscious effort to start praising your children more. Purposely find five things a day you can praise them about. When your daughter dresses up and looks pretty, for example, compliment her. Say, "Oh my, you look beautiful!"

Finally, and most important of all—pray! God will honor your prayers where your children are concerned. Take time daily to pray in faith over them. Take time to declare, "The mercies of God hover over my child! My child is not going to be infected by the drug pushers. My child is going to be able to say, 'No,' because he is a disciple of the Lord, taught by Him, obedient to His Word, and great is his peace!"

Remember this: You can have godly children. God has promised that if you will train up your children in the way they should go, when they are old, they will not depart from it. So get busy training. Get busy planting the seeds of the Word in their heart by teaching them God's principles, setting a pattern for them, being persistent in your faith, participating with them, praising them and praying for them. Give them an inheritance of faith. They will be forever grateful!"

12

When Grown Children Return Back Home

These are different economic times. More than I have ever seen in my lifetime, grown children are returning back home for a variety of reasons and some have never left home. Let's start with the ones who have left and come back. Of course, as parents, the rules are still the same, there are just more when children return because there are different issues and they may come back as parents themselves with your grandchildren. When my daughter returned home and my son had not yet left, I gave them the following contract to sign and it worked! You may devise something similar to your situation and specific issues.

November 14, 2002
<u>Nothing But Love at (Address)!</u>

<u>Control Issues:</u>

(Address)_____ ultimately still belongs to Mother and she has the last say in her house. Mother likes old things.... and she likes to have her things where she leaves them. This is an opportunity for Mother to make deposits in the lives of her daughter, son and grandchildren. Let her do so and listen to your Mother...this is a major opportunity for three grown folks to learn and love from one another at a new level!

Everyone has a job to do, stay FOCUSED and do YOUR Job! WE can help each other and will help each other!

<u>Personal Responsibilities:</u>

<u>Mother</u>
House (upkeep and bills)
Personal Goals for the house for which I will be saving:
> Shed in the back with a lock - April and Phillip to provide
> Upgrade electricity in entire house
> Repair Oven
> Repair furnace in back
> Landscape the front and back of house
> Freezer for the Laundry room
> Work
> Ministry
> Pre and Post-Marital Counseling
> Preaching, Teaching Assignments

<u>April</u>
Work
Care of daughter and son
Paying off bills
School for self

<u>Phillip</u>
Work
Care of daughter
Paying off car note and other bills
School for self

<u>Precious</u>
School
Make up bed...keep room neat, vacuum floor.

One Activity per week – Bible study, or course or fun activity at Sports Complex Center.

Edward
School
Make up bed…keep room neat
Keep toys in room in order
One Activity per week – Bible study, or course or fun activity at Sports Complex Center.

Rent Per Month beginning December 1, 2002:

April, Precious and Ed
Portion for help with utilities/household:
i.e., water, gas, electric, purchase soap, toothpaste and toilet paper)

Phillip
Utilities, gas, electric, purchase soap, toothpaste and toilet paper.

Telephones:
April will get her own telephone. Phillip will get his own telephone beginning December 1, 2002.

NO FEMALES OR MALES ARE ALLOWED TO LOOK AT TV IN ANYONE'S ROOM OR STAY OVERNIGHT IN ANYONE'S ROOM.

Living room is always to be presentable……..neither junky nor messed up. Dust when you see dust piling onto the glass tables. Braiding of hair is to be done in dining room, not in living room and clean up all hair when finished!

Straighten up after yourself in whatever room you use.

Daily Cooking

Sunday	Mother
Monday/Tuesday/Wednesday	April
Thursday/Friday/Saturday	Phillip

Full course meals are expected to be cooked = one meat and two veg-etables. Bread (optional), beverage and dessert. Meals are prepared for the five of us! No excuses for not planning the meals for the days that you are responsible. You do not have to cook all the time….you can have food ordered or delivered for everyone OR YOU CAN TAKE EVERYONE OUT TO DINNER!! No excuses for not planning! On your day to cook, do the dishes and clean kitchen by sweeping, mopping and/or waxing floor. Make sure counter tops are cleaned and dining room or kitchen counter straightened.

If you do not cook or provide food for family for your day........you must take the family out for dinner on your next day. I will be keeping a record. This is simply to build discipline *and* to enhance your cooking skills.

There are volumes of cookbooks in the bookcase in the living room, so select menus and try them.

Bathroom:
Clean up after yourself...wash out the tub directly after your bath and wash tub after showers. Good cleaning of bathroom on the week-ends and re-stock bathroom with toilet paper, soap and tissues. Rotate doing this.

Sunday is the Lord's Day! Everyone is expected to serve God by assembling yourself in a believing church.

Thursday Night is Family Night or Dance Night <u>at home</u>. We will bop or learn it...electric slide, etc. Every one will encircle afterwards and thank God for limbs to dance and for family and any other prayer requests.

You must not leave the house with an attitude........Our serving one another and loving one another should change your attitude.

Vacuum all areas at least once a week! Rotate as needed.

All of our schedules are different...Phillip is working at nights...April is working during week and week–end nights; SUNDAYS.....WE ALL EAT DINNER TOGETHER. THE CHILDREN SHOULD ALWAYS EAT WITH ONE ADULT.

Always remember.....on those days that you don't feel well and don't feel like looking at my face or anybody else's face.....you just want to be left alone........we are family and we love each other....take a warm bubble bath.....close your door and go to bed.

NO Attitudes, no fussing and fighting over telephone, TV....nothing! Life is too short and I do not intend to be a referee. Did that when the two of you were younger! You are adults now~

Babysitting
Let it be known....let it be said.....that Mother is <u>not</u> a live-in babysitter... Please..... just because I am in the house...do not say, Ma watch the baby...I am going out for a minute and come back 2-3 hours later.

Do not say....Ma watch Precious and Ed....going out and will be right back and come back 2-3 hours later. You only have one time to do it and my answer from that point on will be "No." The proper way to do it is, if you know you are going to be out for 2-3 hours, make sure children are fed, homework completed, clothes are ready for the next day. Children have been bathed and are in the bed. Make sure baby is sleep and bottles are ready when he wakes up. Make sure pampers are available for me to change if I have to change while you are gone.

Don't assume....Momma will take care of the kids for me. Doors are opening up for me in the Ministry and I shall walk through them. This is my turn.... help me when you can and support me in the ministry.....I treasure your help! We can make this work.

Signed_____, _____
Date:_____

13

When Parents Go To Live In Their Grown Children's Home

I had the distinct honor of being asked by my son to live with him while I experienced breast cancer. At that particular time in 2007, I remember that my son would come to my home at least three to four times a week at night after he had completed his work on his second job; put out my trash, wash my dishes, straighten up my house and stock my cabinets with food and juices. I knew he was getting tired because several times, I asked him to spend the night in the guest bedroom, because he so was tired and I was afraid he would fall asleep at the wheel on his way home! Finally, he said, "Mom, why don't you come to live with me and I can take better care of you because it is wearing me down coming to your home after I have worked two jobs." Rent this house out, and come and live with me. I said, "Parents don't go to live with their children, children come back and live with their parents." He told me to think about it. I did. I called my Mother the next day and said, "Ma, Phillip asked me to come and live with him so he can take care of me." She said without hesitation, "Louise, Go, go live with Phil, how many children ask their parents to go live with them? That is a blessing. I thought about it for a couple of weeks because I still had that myth in my head that parents do not go to live with their children. I thought about my belongings/furniture and moving.

I had lived in my house for over 14 years. Even though I would have my own bedroom in his home, I still had to downsize a three bedroom house. It was overwhelming. I prayed and thought about it again and decided that if I moved with him and rented out the house, that would be money I could use to pay off my accumulation of $15,000.00 worth of medical bills and I could also help Phillip by paying rent and help him with food, etcera. I finally told him, "Yes, I will move with you and started the process of moving. As I reflect on that move, it was one of the best decisions I have made after accepting Jesus Christ as Lord of my life. He did as he had promised, Phil took "Great" care of me and there was not one day living in Phillip's house that he did not make me laugh! *I never had to buy food*…that was so won-derful and I stayed with him for two years! When I left, all of my medical bills were paid off and I left healed in my body, mind and soul! I slept like a baby every night in his home in my cozy, warm bed. While I was there, I fell and broke my arm and once again, he took care of me. I did not cook for 2 ½ months. He did all the cooking! I do believe my life was lengthened because of the prayers of my family, church family and living in the home of my son. I am a blessed woman!

14

Developmental Stages

The relationship between a father/mother and their daughter and a father/mother and their son is intense, intimate, complex and precious when God controls the reigns! A basic outline of developmental stages will help parents understand the changing needs of young people. These stages have been taken from Lee W. Carlsons' book, "Christian Parenting," pages 57-59.

"Infancy (Birth to crawling or walking)

During this crucial period, the child is forming basic impressions of himself or herself and the world. The baby explores whether to trust or distrust others and his or her feelings. Although the infant can't talk (to be understood). It is critical for people to cuddle the baby and communicate sounds and words. Since babies are born with different temperaments, parents must be flexible to provide different handling and teaching. It is the interaction of temperament and the care received by the baby that has a large impact on an infant's future.

Toddler hood (Walking to age two)

This is the age of exploration, which results in the learning of self-confidence or self-doubt. Newly acquired movement and articulation skills lead to the urge to try out everything in the environment. Therefore, by childproofing the house or by constant "no-no's."

First Adolescence (The terrible twos)

This is a transitional phase marked by the word "No!" In exploring his or her sense of independence, the child is moving toward either self-identity or social conforming. The two-years-old's sense of self depends on rebelling against (testing) the parental will in order to try out his or her own will.

Parental responses are important. Continually negative responses can help form depressed, defeated children. Can't you ever do anything right?" is a familiar parental attitude that, when repeated often, will eat away at a child's sense of worth. Or, a spoiled brat may result when parents constantly coddle or protect a child.

In contrast, frequent positive comments and expressions of love that affirm a child will tend to produce a confident, communicative child. A loving hug and comments like, "You did a good job!" are helpful parental responses.

Preschool (Ages three to five)

This is a time of relative stability, while many developmental processes are occurring, such as:

a. building physical skills and motor coordination
b. controlling impulses (like grabbing a toy from another child)
c. reducing dependence on mother
d. learning to relate to other children
e. learning to express feelings appropriately
f. developing sex-role identity as male or female
g. responding to intellectual stimulation

Although ups and downs occur, age four can be as unstable as age two sometimes, growth in confidence and self-assurance usually mark this stage.

Middle Childhood (Ages six to eleven)

During this period, the family gradually loses some of its influence because school teachers, and peers become more important to the child. The child's world is rapidly expanding. Still dependent on self-confidence and emotional support from home, the child is learning a sense of mastery or a sense of inadequacy to meet the multiple demands of the environment. It is a time when the child is reaching out for independence while still clinging to family for nurturance and support.

Preadolescence (Approximately ages eleven to thirteen)

The upheaval that will establish the child's adult identity begins in preadolescence. It is a stage of disorganization marked by rebellion (like first adolescence). Among both girls and boys, physical changes may cause confusion ("What's happening to me?") and phases of moodiness ('If I feel miserable, I'll make sure others do too'). The task of the preadolescent is to tear down his or her childhood identity and to begin building an adult identity. Rules and authority are often abhorred, and the accompanying tirades sometimes seem incomprehensible to bewildered parents.

Early Adolescence (Puberty to age fifteen)

The search for adult identity continues, complicated by the sometimes-unsettling changes of puberty. The defiance of adult authority may increase, and yet the criticalness carried over from preadolescence serves to encourage the independent thinking necessary for forming a mature identity. Questioning of traditional values and rules by the young person, when handled with give-and take dialogue and communication (listening) by parents, can also further the young person's identity formation as an adult. For many youth, peer pressure is the most important reality.

Late Adolescence (Ages sixteen to twenty-one)

The balance is tipped toward independent thinking and living during this stage. Criticalness becomes tempered and aimed at peers as well as parents. Some of the tasks at this time are exploring vocational goals, establishing ethical priorities, and working on sexual maturity.

During these latter two stages, a youth must accomplish the task of forming an identity that is different from his or her parents. The task of emerging as a self-determining adult, able to give love and receive love in return, is characterized

by the persistent struggle between independence and dependence, between security and
insecurity.

In reading the above general developmental
stage patterns for each year, realize that each
child is different and may not display every char-
acteristic, but this is a guide. Our children are
special, they are the hope of the world and we
must prepare them to be contributing members
of society, who understand natural laws and the
principles of life.

"Children will rise up against parents." This
passage brings you in remembrance of the adolescence stages and the "attitudes" adolescents
have. Bad attitudes are destructive and disrespectful, adolescents need to be shown that they
are in charge of those attitudes. Yes, it is okay to
disagree with what the adolescent has been told
to do or not to do, but how do they disagree and
in what tone? Go and do what was told of you to
do and then let's talk! Maybe there can be some
compromising and negotiation and maybe not.
Let's talk.

Bad attitudes are a sign that something is
wrong. Is it anger, bitterness, unforgiveness or
defiant behavior? Does it feel like you are bat-
tling your child? Do you like your child? Can you
believe that this is your child? This is a trying and
difficult time for parents, but the key is endurance." Obey God and teach your children His
Word, His precepts, His statues and judgments.

We must do as Deuteronomy 6:7-9 says,

> "And you shall teach them diligently
> to your sons and shall talk of them
> when you sit in your house and when
> you walk by the way and when you lie
> down and when you rise up.
>
> And you shall bind them as a sign on
> your hand and they shall be as fron-
> tals on your forehead. And you shall
> write them on the doorposts of your
> house and on your gates."

The aim is to train and mold self-governing children who choose the proper way. We must be able to give personally to our children what we preach and teach. What we do, speaks louder than what we say. When they see that what we say, lines up with what we do, we become effective."

David and Virginia Edens state,

> "When children see their parents prac-
> ticing Christianity in everyday tasks
> and experiences, then Christianity
> begins to have meaning for them.
>
> Parents who show that they hold
> Christ in high esteem by taking active

part in the life of the church illustrate Christianity to their children in a way that needs no text. God gave children parents for a purpose. He expects parents to provide for them physically, to love and discipline them intelligently, and to set before them worthy examples. As parents meet these needs, they have the assurance that "great shall be the peace of thy children." Isaiah 54:13

Talk with your child as well as spend meaningful and purposeful time. Go on individual dates with your children to show them that they are special. Begin to be a part of some of the activities they enjoy.

15

Violence...Thou Shall Not Kill!

God states it very clear in the ten commandments listed in the King James Version of the Bible in Exodus, right after the 5th commandment "Honour thy father and mother that thy days be long in the land which the Lord gives thee" is the 6th commandment; "Thou Shalt Not Kill." Today, we have policemen shooting our children like they are play toys. We still have "black on black" crimes. There are consequences when you are disobedient to God's Commandments.....grieve, fear, hurt, pain and suffering. A father and mother is grieving right now as I speak over the lost of their son. The latest victim is a teenager, Michael Brown in Ferguson, Missouri. My heart is hurting for the parents and I am angry at our society. The job of a policeman is to protect, but the autopsy shows that the teenager was shot six times, twice to the head. Yes, Michael Brown was big for his age, intimidating to the policeman and had just robbed a store in a video before the shooting, but Michael Brown was unarmed and his hands were raised in the air surrendering, however, it did not make a difference. I believe that the intention was to kill him, not stop him. Sad to say, but many of our police officers are scared and their motto seems to be, "let me get them before they get me." This kind of violence must stop! An article updated by Amanda Taub on November 26, 2014 in Voxmedia.com entitled, "The Real Scandal of Police Violence in Ferguson is What's Legal" is stated as follows:

"A grand jury has decided that Ferguson, Missouri, police office Darren Wilson will not face charges for killing Michael Brown.

For many who wanted Wilson to be punished for Brown's death, it's a scandal that Wilson has gotten away with what they see as a crime. But the bigger scandal is that what he did arguably wasn't a crime at all. Our legal standards and legal system make it difficult — if not impossible — to prosecute police violence.

It was never likely that Wilson would be prosecuted for shooting Brown. The set of situations in which police officers are allowed to use force is narrow in theory, but broad in application.

Police officers are not allowed to use deadly force except in a few theoretically narrow circumstances: in defense of themselves or others, or to prevent a suspect from fleeing the scene of a "dangerous felony."

That sounds quite limiting — and it would be if the danger had to actually be real or the dangerous felony had to have actually taken place. But that's not the law. What matters, legally, is whether the officer *reasonably believed* that those factors were present — or can convince a jury that he did.

And that's not hard to do, because police officers are given a great deal of deference by the legal system. Juries tend to perceive police officers as credible, and so are likely to credit officers' claims that their fear was reasonable.

And race adds a thumb on the scale: Americans overestimate black people's involvement in crime, which is helpful to an officer trying to claim that he believed a black victim was a threat, as has been the case in so many high-profile police shootings.

That means that to press criminal charges in a police shooting, the prosecutor has a heavy burden to overcome. The officer is likely to claim that he believed the suspect was a threat and made a split-second decision to use force. The jury is likely to believe him, even if his decision was a bad one.

That makes it difficult for the justice system to hold police officers to accountability when they use force against people who didn't actually pose a threat at all. We don't know exactly how often police officers shoot people who turn out to be unarmed, because there isn't any reliable data on police killings. But every Michael Brown, John Crawford, or Tamir Rice is a reminder that that happens far too often."

We must begin to teach our children how to act and react when a policeman stops our children, especially if they are Black males. I have given my son survival tactics and rules repeatedly, especially when he was younger, "Do not talk back and talk smart to policemen, be cordial and polite if you are driving and they stop you and do what they tell you to do, do not raise your voice and look at their badges to see a name and badge number and memorize it if anything happens." I wanted my son to live and to be honest, he never believed that he would live to graduate from high school. He now has a college degree and his own business! Prayer, survival tactics and rules work....when your children use them, but you must teach them, so that your children can use them!

I have taken excerpts from the August 21, 2014 article entitled, "What Black Parents Tell Their Sons About the Police" written by Jazmine Hughes in Gawker.com and she presents it this way:

"At what age is a black boy when he learns, he's scary?

This question retains its relevance now more than ever. Some have called Michael Browns' killing and the newly newsworthy manifestation of systemic racism and state-sanctioned brutality against black men, a reproductive issue, arguing that it prevents women and men from their right "to parent the children we have in safe and healthy environments:" It makes people afraid to have black babies, because they won't stand a chance. As a black woman, nothing will stop me from bearing and raising my future child, but nothing will stop me from raising them in fear.

Such is the burden of black parenting. Being a black parent, especially of a black boy, comes with the added onus of having to protect your child from a country that is out to get him—a country that kills someone that looks like him every 28 hours, a country that will likely imprison him by his mid-thirties, if he doesn't get his high school diploma, a country that is more than twice as likely to suspend him from school than a white classmate.

This fear has fueled a generational need for a portentous, culturally compulsory lecture that warns young black men about the inherent strikes against them, about the society that is built to bring them down. It is a harbinger of the inevitable, a wishful attempt at exceptionalism, passed down like an heirloom.

Every black male I've ever met has had this talk, and it's likely that I'll have to give it one day too. There are so many things I need to tell my future son, already, before I've birthed him; so many innocuous, trite thoughts that may not make a single difference. *Don't wear a hoodie. Don't try to break up a fight. Don't talk back to cops. Don't ask for help.* But they're all variations of a single theme: *Don't give them an excuse to kill you."*

Parents: What would you have told Michael Brown before he left the house on that particular day?

Begin to tell it to your children....everyday, so that it becomes ingrained in their spirits."

16

Faith and Discipline

To paraphrase how the Bible says it best in Galatians 5:6, genuine faith works through love. It is difficult to have faith and not be connected by love. According to Migliore, "A Christian's victorious love at work in Jesus' ministry, cross, and resurrection showing us that this is God's way of life, "loving is greater than any other plan we could come up with."

Jim Larson discusses in his book, "Growing a Healthy Family" on page 90 about the value of faith and why faith is essential as follows:

1. "Faith provides a framework for dealing with the perplexities of life. There certainly are rights and wrongs in life, but increasingly there seem to be many "in-betweens' that can make us feel confused or upset.

Faith can give us understanding and direction for confronting these difficulties.

2. Faith can give us a sense of inner peace. In encountering conflicts in our families and elsewhere, we may find ourselves exhausted or burned out from trying to resolve these difficulties. Our faith can give us a feeling of peace, a sense of relief. Faith brings comfort.

3. Faith can give us power to face our difficulties. A vibrant faith can give people courage to deal with what may at times seem overwhelming. It brings power to grapple with life. We know that we are not alone. We believe that there is a God who hears, understands, and is with us in whatever happens.

4. Faith can motivate us to develop relationships with other people. There is value in having friendships outside the family as well. To expect our families to meet all of our emotional and relational needs is to place an enormous and unrealistic burden on them.

Committing ourselves to a growing faith will bring us into contact with persons who share similar beliefs and values. This may happen through a structured organization such as a church, or a more unstructured group of friends we develop on our own.

Such relationships can be helpful in creating a support network, persons with whom we can share, those who will encourage and support us in times of personal and family difficulties.

Children must have something and someone to trust and believe in and God will meet this need when parents fail. Children's faith will help them better understand and eventually help them to forgive their parents."

Katherine Kersey in her book, "The Art of Sensitive Parenting" says:

"Children must learn from their mistakes, like the rest of us. But if parents are willing to give up some of their control, keep the lines of communication open, and still make their expectations clear and reasonable, the mistakes their children make will not have to be so drastic, nor leave such permanent scars."

"Treat your child with respect. We must imitate the nursing mother the Bible talks about in 1 Thessalonians 2:7, regarding how the nursing mother tenderly cares for her own children and we must care for our own as such.

Many of us have inherited a disrespectful attitude toward our children. We nag them, demand from them, embarrass them, and command them. If we repeatedly talk down to the child, we begin to build a wall that separates us. Our children begin to not want us in his/her world anymore. They shut us out. Others can come in, but not us, because the wall is so high and is filled with so many hurts. Do we like to be bossed around or embarrassed? Their response is the same as ours, because if we are treated that way, our normal response is negative. "Forget it!" "No Way!" "I don't want to!" "You do it!" "You can't make me do it!" The price is high when we put our children down.

We must respect our children as persons to help them feel that they are just as important as others. They are not equals, but they are important. Faith and discipline go hand in hand. Hebrews 11 speaks of faith and Hebrews 12 speaks of discipline. Every father who truly loves his son disciplines him."

The Bible talks about the discipline of a Father in Hebrews 12:5-9: (New American Standard Version)

"And you have forgotten the exhortation which is addressed to you as sons, my son, do not regard lightly the discipline of the Lord. Nor faint when you are reproved by Him; for those whom the Lord loves He disciplines and He scourges every son whom He receives.

"It is for discipline that you endure; God deals with you as with sons; for what son is there whom his father does not discipline? But if you are without discipline, of which all have become partakers, then you are illegitimate children and not sons.

Furthermore, we had earthly fathers to discipline us, and we respected them: shall we not much rather be subject to the Father of spirits, and live?"

Discipline is not the same as punishment. To grow into mature, responsible and well-adjusted adults, children need discipline. They must be taught that they cannot display unacceptable behaviors. According to Webster, "Discipline is training which corrects, molds, strengthens, or perfects." Punishment is one form of discipline. We all want to raise happy children who are responsible, self-controlled, who possess self-respect and show respect for others. We want our children to be educated and to develop every talent and gift God gave them. It is clear that the purpose of discipline is not simply saying "No" and directing. Discipline teaches respect and sets reasons for limits providing controls for children.

Now that we have talked about discipline, how do we instill it in our children? How does it happen? Parents must learn techniques, good parenting skills. We cannot raise children the way we were raised if our parents' methods in our upraising were too authoritative or too permissive.

In the "ABC's of Parenting," Joan Barbuto talks about using authoritative or permissive methods of child raising and she states,

"In fact, by using such methods they may even harm them psychologically. From the evidence in our country today, many parents do not know how to deal with their children. There were more than 2.7 million reports of child abuse in 1992, according to the National Center for the Prevention of Child Abuse. Alcoholism and drug abuse are widespread among teenagers, teenage pregnancy is a major problem, and mental illness is increasing in children. The International Congress of Pediatrics predicted several years ago that the main health problems children will have in the future will be emotional, not physical."

"Even today, one of seven children suffers from mental illness, and four out of five children with mental illness receive no care or inadequate care, according to a National Mental Health Association Study. It is estimated that 1.8 percent of children, seven to 12 suffer from depression. Although some children may have a genetic vulnerability to depression, environmental stress generally triggers it, according to child specialists."

Many children are troubled and get into trouble because they have parents who do not care, are on drugs, mentally ill, or are abusive. Yet on the other hand, many troubled children have parents who love them, but some parents have not yet found the balance in managing their children.

So our children grow up irresponsible and rebellious. Some parents have taken the initiative to get help, but the parents who really need the parenting the most do not realize they need help and do not seek it.

You may be reading this section and know that you are or may have been a parent who has abused or neglected your child or someone else's child. You may feel down, frustrated, overwhelmed and depressed with the care of your own children right now. Please do not be afraid to call someone. Seek the counsel of your Pastor or the Elders in your church. Child Protective Services are not _only_ in place to take your children away, but they have family services to assist you.

Ask to open up a "family services case" D. C. (202) 671-7233, District of Columbia Child Abuse Hotline; Prince Georges' County Screening Unit for Child and Adult Protective Services Maryland, (301) 909-2450, Virginia (703) 838-0800, Virginia Abuse and Neglect State Hotline for Children and Adults; or in any State, dial 211 and speak to an Information and Referral Counselor for family crisis, loss of job, need for food or clothing. If there is an emergency in your family and a life is in danger, please call 911. Family Crisis Center of Prince Georges' 24 hour Hotline (301) 731-1203 or for non-emergency support or information, (301) 779-2100. Find the nearest family service center in your state.

17

Yes Sir, No Sir, Yes Ma'am, No Ma'am and Other Manners!

I was raised to say "Yes Sir, No Ma'am, Yes Ma'am and No Ma'am!" Even though my teachers, beginning in elementary school always told me to say, "Yes" and "No," I said it only to them because they told me to, but many times, I slipped and said to my teachers what my mother taught me, Yes and No Ma'am.

Several times, I slipped at home and said, "Yes" or "No" to my mother and she was not having it and said so! She told me, "You say to your teachers what they tell you to say, but when you come home…make the switch!" I learned fast where to say what. My mother passed to be with the Lord at almost 80 years old and I was still saying, Yes Ma'am and No Ma'am to her before she passed. I taught my children and now my grandchildren to say the same. For me, it meant and still does means, Respect! Merriam Webster defines respect as "a feeling of admiring someone or something that is good, valuable, important, a feeling or understanding that someone or something is important, serious and should be treated in an appropriate way; a particular way of thinking about or looking at something."

We live in a high technology world where we must look for ways to bring back manners and respect that is considered old fashion. June Hines Moore in her book, "You Can Raise a Well-Mannered Child" says it this way in her chapter entitled, "Where Have All The Manners Gone?"

"Perhaps they disappeared along with family values. One thing we do know: Rules of common courtesy are hardly ever taught in our public school today, even though many teachers would, if they could. Also, children do not inherit good manners. They get them by growing up with parents who model and teach them. We might say that home is the classroom where students study their parents. How did we plummet from "Please" and "Thank you" to "Yuk" and "Gimme"?

Parents are not necessarily at fault. Since the fifties, our society has forced the proverbial pendulum to swing to the extreme. In less than a decade, we went from the silver spoon mentality prevalent in the early part of this century to the hippies and free love of the sixties and seventies. That generation questioned the values and more of the establishment. In most circles since then, the prevailing attitude has been "Do your own thing," If it feels good, do it," and "I'm not responsible." We find ourselves struggling to return to a more considerate and responsible society.

By the nineties, we grew tired of the rudeness and crudeness. Actually, the corporate world noticed that young professionals were so socially inept, they threatened the balance sheet. Business was lost because their highly skilled and well-educated young men and women chewed gum, neglected to introduce people and stuffed their mouths with food while they tried to make the big sale over lunch with a client.

Corporations began seeking etiquette trainers and consultants to come in to smooth out the rough edges. Because money often motivates us where nothing else will, desperate executives are forcing the pendulum to swing the other way. We call it customer service. Of course, manners were originally God's idea. He gave us the Golden rule which says we should treat others as we like to be treated. Today business publications of all kinds refer to the same rule we see in Matthew 7:12 and Luke 6:31.

Television still makes its contribution to the demise of socially acceptable behavior with popular comedy shows where the only polite person is a geek. The family with strong moral values is almost nonexistent on many programs. Even commercials for family shows advertise bad manners. Much of the rude behavior that we see in our children surfaces simply because they do not know the proper thing to do. It is that simple and that sad.

Our children deserve the opportunity to learn. We teach out of love and obedience to God's Word that tells us to nurture our children and build godly character in them. Showing consideration for others is part of that. Luke says that "Jesus grew...in favor with God and men' (Luke 2:52, NIV). The Bible does not give us Mary and Joseph's parenting plan, but it does say that with every charge or promise, God shows us the way."

June Hines Moore further asks the questions: "Why is it so important that we direct our children in the way they should go? Why can't we just let them make their own choices, which usually do not include showing consideration for anyone's needs, but their own? Perhaps the answer lies in knowing that everything from plants to people grow in the direction we plant them.

Plants and children have a lot in common. Both grow in the direction that best meets their needs. When we turn a child toward God, he grows spiritually. When we turn him toward the way of the world, we take a quantum leap chance. A plant grows toward the sun because its sustenance and growth must come from it. Our children will grow in the wrong direction, away from God, unless we teach them early that God alone will sustain them and meet their needs. They need a strong early start, not just attending church to find the Lord, but seeing Him everyday at home and in the lives of their parents who model good manners and reveal a personal relationship with the Lord. Spiritually, our children grow in the direction we point them. Will they grow straight or crooked? Like a tree, influences and forces mold a child from within. Someone compared a child to a piece of clay that we mold with our hands. But clay does not grow; clay is molded entirely from without. A child grows and matures from within and is more like a living plant that bears fruit, sometimes sweet and sometimes sour. Social skills learned at home and at church produce the fruits of the Spirit listed in Galatians 5: love, joy, peace, patience, kindness, goodness, faithfulness, gentleness and self-control. Teaching a child confidence in interpersonal skills can open doors to making friends, witnessing and sharing God's Word.

Scripture affirms that *"Jesus grew in wisdom and stature and in favor with God and men"* (Luke 2:52, NIV). His parents pointed Him in the right direction from His youth. They took Him to the temple and no doubt taught Him at home. *According to the Wycliffe Bible Commentary,* Jesus was not a child prodigy in the sense that He was abnormal. He had to mature and learn just as every child does today! He even had to learn manners; yet He was perfect in every stage as He reached it. Another biblical portrait of a child *"growing...in favor both with the Lord and with men* is young Samuel (1 Samuel 2:26). His mother, Hannah, dedicated him to God before he was born. After Hannah nurtured and taught him, she kept her vow and took him to live at the temple. We know that Samuel became a great judge of the nation, Israel. Just as God chose Hannah, He chooses us to raise a specific child, whether we raise him or her in a two-parent home, a single-parent home, or in a grandparent's home. John 15:16 says, "You did not choose Me, but I chose you, and appointed you, that you should go and bear fruit and that your fruit should remain."

If God gives us children, he gives us our most important and challenging fruit crop. We call it parenting. However, just as no two families are identical, no two children are alike; therefore, we look for different way of interacting to be effective. Children have "felt" needs for parents to discover. We see those needs by watching for signs and observing their responses and reactions to see what makes them feel good about themselves and their accomplishments.

In the Seibert family, Jeremy is reserved and introspective. John craves attention. No one would call him a loner. Just as these two guys react differently to people, they have different "felt" needs because they have different personalities. Jeremy's need may include striving for perfection. John may be interested in learning manners only if he can do it while having fun with his friends. He needs social interaction. An old adage says, we can change the set of the sail, but not the wind. We can change methods with Jeremy and John, but we should not try to change their natural bent. Yes, you *can* raise a well-mannered child without losing your own p's and q's, or your child. Learning manners can and should be fun. Children often think their parents spend hours dreaming up a bunch of silly rules, just to lecture them and make their lives miserable. Once they learn there is a reason for every rule of etiquette and that their lives can be more fun and comfortable, they are eager—well, maybe not eager, but more willing---to practice good social skills."

June Moore discusses, <u>Appropriate Manners to Rude People</u>:

- "First, we must remember that some people have never had the opportunity to learn simple social skills. Though we think the rules are just common sense, we must realize that some offenders do not mean to misbehave. They often change their conduct when they redden with embarrassment.
- If someone nearby disturbs you, say, 'I am sorry, but I can't hear the performance." Returning rude for rude usually elicits more of the same. If the noise continues, you may ask an usher to call the manager. The alternative is to move to another available seat.

- One etiquette authority says staring "more-in-pity-than-in anger" at the perpetrator is often the most effective way.
- If someone is seated in your assigned place, check your ticket stub and quietly say, "I believe you are sitting in our seats." If the intruder refuses to move, or if you have trouble finding occupied seats, return to the usher for assistance. Other members of your party should wait at the back of the auditorium until you have secured seating space.

Psalm 139:13-18 describes how each child, unique in God's creation, is *"fearfully and wonderfully" made*. When we discover a child's natural bent, we usually find that child's felt need. Then we are on our way to raising children who are in favor with God and man."

18

Education is The Answer

STRATEGIC PLAN:
COURSES/WORKSHOPS FOR PARENTING

There is a wealth of material available for parents. Education will make the difference. The following is a strategic goal setting plan for courses/workshops for parents which will soon be implemented. These basic courses/workshops will be practical, supportive, life-changing, and transform your parenting skills. They will cover the following areas:

- Instructions/Tools on Becoming the Better Parent Your Child Needs.
- Stages and Ages – Diving into Child Development.
- Assertive Communication for Parents.

- From Anger and Conflict.....to Cooperation.
- Step-Parenting Dynamics.
- Parenting Mistakes.
- Discipline for Children, Gain Respect from Your Children
- Faith Parenting.
- Relationship With Your Children.
- Establishing a Happy, Peaceful Family Life.
- Stress Management.
- Establishing Structure in Daily Routines.
- Advice and Tips to Single Fathers/Mothers.
- Establish Family Goals.
- Going Down Your Family Memory Lane – Reflections!
- What....The Book of Proverbs?
- Fathers....Not In Place!
- Build an Inheritance for Your Children.
- Tools to Expose Children to Reading ....Early!
- Gain Less Talk-back, Less Nagging and Less Fighting.
- Exploring Your Family's' World, Goals and Needs
- Role Playing – Deepening Your Listening Skills.
- Role Playing – How to Give Your Child Quality, Positive Feedback.
- Removing Unhealthy Patterns of Parenting.
- Role Playing: Co-parenting Communication.

- Are My Children Watching Too Much TV and Spending Too Much Time on Social Media? (Learning the different Social Medias)
- Developing Healthy Self-Esteem.
- Money, Allowances, Instilling Positive Work Ethics.
- School and Home Violence.
- Discussing Tough Topics, Smoking, Drugs, Rape, Sexual Orientation, Death, Divorce, Worrying, Sickness, Puberty, Menstruation, Stealing, Lying, Strangers, Wellness and Bullying.
- Discussing Your Teen Having a Baby.
- Role Playing to *Better* Your Overall Parenting Skills.
- Building Traditions: Making Holidays Less Materialistic.

19

Teaching About Money/ Instilling Positive Work Ethics

I know how to stretch a dollar; my mother taught and showed me how.

When I was 10 years old, we lived in the projects of Washington, D. C. on Atlantic Street, Southeast. At the bottom of the hill was a grocery store. My mother would always give me a list and the money to purchase milk, bread, can goods, etc. She loved cashew nuts, so they were on the list, many times. My mother worked hard, but she usually had more items on the list than she gave me money for. I remember the first time she sent me to the store and there were 2-3 items that I was not able to purchase. When I came home without the items and a few coins of change left, I noticed she was upset, but more importantly, I noticed she was not specifically angry at me. She knew that she had not given me enough money to buy all the items on the list. I told myself that the next time she sent me to the store; I would shop better and get everything on the list she wanted. I highly respected my mother; because she worked long hours, six days a week managing a dry cleaning business which did not pay very much.

The next time I went to the store, I counted the money she gave me and looked at my list. When I arrived at the store, I bought all off brand names in order to get everything on the list. I added each item to make sure I had enough money to cover everything. When I came into the house with everything on the list and a few coins of change left, placing it in her hand, she was so happy. She was all smiles. She did not care that many of the items I purchased were brands we had never heard of! She didn't even look at the store receipt.

I learned a wonderful lesson. I loved the candy that came in a box called, "good and plenty." After shopping for the family on a regular basis, I decided now that my mother had firmly entrusted me with making the right decisions in purchasing our food. I decided that I would add my "good and plenty's" to the list….in my head, of course. I never told her. I would get everything on the list and also include my "good and plenty's" as my payment for going to the store. I ate and enjoyed the "good and plenty's" on the way home and threw away the box before I got home.

She never looked at the grocery receipt, because she now knew that I always got everything on the list! I began to enjoy going to the store for my Mother! I never had an attitude when she asked me; in fact, I knew I was going to get a treat each time I ran down the hill to the grocery store! I was so happy! I had learned how to take care of my family's need and mine too!

I remember when we lived in Albuquerque, New Mexico and I bought both of my children piggy banks to place on their dressers and taught them how to save at very young ages. Phillip was 7 and April was 12, I took them to the bank, introduced them to my banker and the bank personnel and we opened their own individual savings accounts. They each received an allowance, had to save 10% and pay 10% to our church for tithes. I provided them the tithing envelopes and watched them fill it out and held the tithing envelopes in my Bible and gave them their envelopes on Sunday to place in the offering plates.

I also taught them how to fill out their deposit slips and I took them to the bank to make monthly deposits in their savings accounts. I checked their accounts on a monthly basis to make sure all transactions were properly recorded. Both accounts should always have the same amount because they both received the same amount for their allowance.

After about 6 months into our saving, I noticed April's account had less than Phillip's and noticed that there had been withdrawals from her account. I asked her what she spent the money on and how was she able to withdraw the money without my consent. She stated she brought snacks, bought her friend a birthday present and a card and bought her teacher a present! She also stated that the Banker I introduced her to, she went directly to her to withdraw the money, so she did not have to show identification!

Never in my wildest dreams did I think she would go into the bank by herself and withdraw money. I was impressed and told her so, because she used the skills I had taught her, but I was able to address another issue with her; yes, this is your savings account, but we must discuss your purchases first. I did not have to address that issue again. I said to myself, this girl is smart!

Laura Chin, Writing Contributor to Forbes' column; Personal Finance in her article dated, October 15, 2013, entitled, "The 5 Most Important Money Lessons to Teach Your Kids" says it this way:

"Given how important financial skills are to navigating life, it's surprising that our schools don't teach children about money.

As a parent, however, you can teach your child important financial lessons — and you should.

"Look at the mortgage crisis and how many families lost their homes — 3.9 million foreclosures. Look at the amount of money — $1.1 trillion—we owe in student loan debt. The amount

— $845 billion — we owe in credit card debt. It's pretty clear that adults don't know much about money. To help the next generation avoid the mistakes of their elders, and to live financially fit lives, they need to be taught the essentials about money," says Beth Kobliner, author of the *New York Times* bestseller, <u>*Get a Financial Life*</u>, and a Member of the President's Advisory Council on Financial Capability who spearheaded the creation of <u>*Money as You Grow*</u>, which offers age-appropriate money lessons for children.

Kobliner says children as young as three years old can grasp financial concepts like saving and spending. And a report by researchers at the University of Cambridge commissioned by the United Kingdom's Money Advice Service revealed that kids' money habits are formed by age 7."

"The sooner parents start taking advantage of everyday teachable money moments (for example, give a six-year-old $2 and let her choose which fruit to buy), the better off our kids will be. Parents are the number one influence on their children's financial behaviors, so it's up to us to raise a generation of mindful consumers, investors, savers, and givers," she says.

Below are the top money lessons to be learned at each age, as well as activities to illustrate each point.

"Ages 3-5

The Lesson: You may have to wait to buy something you want. "This is a hard concept for people to learn of all ages," says Kobliner. However, the ability to delay gratification can also predict how successful one will be as a grown-up. Kids at this age need to learn that if they really want something, they should wait and save to buy it.

Money lessons at this age set the tone for later on. "You really can't start too early," says Kobliner. Speaking of her own family, she says, "When we go into a store, if I say, 'We don't have money for this,' they're smart — they know we have credit cards," So, she would say, "We're here to buy a gift for X, and we're not going to buy anything for you, because we're not here for that." Kids then quickly learn that going into a store doesn't always mean you'll buy something.

Activities For Ages 3 To 5

1. When your child is waiting in line, say, to go on the swings, discuss how important it is to learn to wait for what he or she wants.

2. Create three jars – each labeled "Saving," "Spending" or "Sharing." Every time your child receives money, whether for doing chores or from a birthday, divide the money equally among the jars. Have him or her use the spending jar for

small purchases, like candy or stickers. Money in the sharing jar can go to someone you know who needs it or be used to donate to a friend's cause. The saving jar should be for more expensive items.

3. Have your child set a goal, such as to buy a toy. Make sure it's not so pricey that they won't be able to afford it for months. "Then it just gets frustrating, and it gets hard for them to wrap their head around. It's really more about her being cognizant that she's saving for a goal than, 'Oh, I really need her to scrape together $10 to buy the tutu.' You want to set them up for success," says Kobliner. If your child does have an expensive goal, come up with a matching program to help her reach it in a reasonable timeframe. (Kobliner says that while an allowance is a personal choice for every family, at this age, a small allowance could help a child save for these goals.)

Every time your child adds money to the savings jar, help her count up how much she has, talk with her about how much she needs to reach her goal, and when she will reach it. "All those behaviors are really fun for kids," says Kobliner. "And it gives them a sense of the importance of waiting and being patient and saving."

Ages 6-10

The Lesson: You need to make choices about how to spend money. At this age, it's important to explain to your child, "Money is finite and it's important to make wise choices, because once you spend the money you have, you don't have more to spend," Kobliner says. While at this age, you should also keep up with activities like the saving, spending and sharing jars, and goal-setting, you should also begin to engage your child in more adult financial decision-making.

Activities For Ages 6 To 10

1. Include your child in some financial decisions. For instance, explain, "The reason I chose the generic grape juice rather than the brand name is that it costs 50 cents less and tastes the same to me," says Kobliner. Or talk about deals, such as buying everyday staples like paper towels in bulk to get a cheaper per-item price.

2. Give your child some money, like $2, in a supermarket and have her make choices about what fruit to buy, within the parameters of what you need, to give them the experience of making choices with money.

3. When you're shopping, talk aloud about how you're making your financial decisions as a grown-up, asking questions like, "Is this something we really, really need? Or can we skip it this week since we're going out to dinner?" "Can I borrow it?" "Would it cost less somewhere else? Could we go to discount store and get two of these instead of one?"

<u>Ages 11-13</u>

The Lesson: The sooner you save, the faster your money can grow from compound interest. At this age, you can shift from the idea of saving for short-term goals to long-term goals. Introduce the concept of compound interest, when you earn interest both on your savings as well as on past interest from your savings.

<u>Activities For Ages 11 To 13</u>

1. Describe compound interest using specific numbers, because research shows this is more effective than describing it in the abstract, says Kobliner. Explain, "If you set aside $100 every year starting at age 14, you'd have $23,000 by age 65, but if you start at age 35, you'll only have $7,000 by age 65."

2. Have your child do some compound interest calculations on Investor.gov. Here, she can see how much money she'll earn if she invests a certain amount and it grows by a certain interest rate. And have her read this inspiring example of someone who used compound interest to his advantage incredibly well.

3. Have your child set a longer-term goal for something more expensive than the toys she may have been saving for. "Those sorts of tradeoffs, called opportunity costs — what are the things you're giving up to save money — is a very useful

thing to talk about. At this age, kids are trying to *not* save because they want to buy stuff, but thinking of what long-term goals are and what they're having to give up shows that it's a good decision," says Kobliner. For example, she says, if your child has a habit of buying a snack after school every day, she may decide she'd rather put that money toward an iPod.

Ages 14-18

The Lesson: When comparing colleges, be sure to consider how much each school would cost. Search for the "net price calculator" on college websites to see how much each costs when including other expenses besides tuition. But don't let the price tag discourage your child. Explain how much more college grads earn than people without college degrees, making it a worthwhile investment.

Activities For Ages 14 To 18

1. Discuss how much you can contribute to your child's college education each year. "Every parent should start the college cost conversation by ninth grade," says Kobliner. "Tackling the subject early and being honest about what your family can afford will help kids be realistic about where they may apply."

But remember that there are many ways to finance college other than with your own money. With your child, look into which private schools are generous with financial aid, how much of it is in "free money" such as grants and scholarships, how much in loans that your child will have to pay back, and what government programs can help pay back those loans, says Kobliner. Also, check out these eight tips on taking out student loans.

2. Have your child use a College Scorecard to compare how much each college costs, what the employment prospects of graduates are, and how much student loan debt could affect your child's lifestyle after graduation, if he or she attended that college. As with any investment, analyze together whether the money put in will pay off in the end.

3. Estimate your financial aid using the FAFSA4caster tool at fafsa.ed.gov. Also research additional loans, scholarships, and grants — and use calculators to estimate monthly loan payments — on studentaid.ed.gov. Find out about loan repayment options such as Pay As You Earn, which limits your monthly payments to just 10% of your discretionary income. For more information, check out ibrinfo.org or finaid.org.

"Parents should absolutely make their college kids get a part-time job," says Kobliner, adding that research by Dr. Gary R. Pike of Indiana University-Purdue University Indianapolis shows that students who work 20 hours a week or less at on-campus jobs get better grades because they're more engaged in student life. "But limit those hours!" she says. "Working more than 20 hours per week can hurt kids' academic success."

Ages 18+

The Lesson: You should use a credit card only if you can pay the balance off in full each month.

It is all too easy to slide into credit card debt, which could give your child the burden of paying off credit card debt at the same time as student loans. Plus, it could affect his or her credit history, which could make it difficult to, say, buy a car or a home, or even to get a job. Sometimes, prospective employers check credit.

"The average household owes $7,084 in credit card debt. To reverse the trend of spending beyond our means and racking up hundreds of dollars a year in interest, it's critical that parents teach their kids how to use credit cards responsibly (or better yet—not at all!—unless they can pay the total bill every month)," says Kobliner.

Activities For Ages 18+

1. Teach a child that if a parent cosigns on a credit card, any late payment could also affect the parent's credit history.

2. Together, look for a credit card that offers a low interest rate and no annual fee using sites like Bankrate, Creditcards.com, Credit.com, or Cardratings.com.

3. Explain that it's important not to charge everyday items, so that way, if you have an emergency expense that you can't cover with savings, you can charge that. However, even better is building up at least three months' worth of living expenses in emergency savings, though six to nine months' worth is ideal. Learn here how to budget money in order to build up emergency savings."

I saw my Mother work hard and sacrifice for us, therefore, I became a hard worker and sacrificed for my children. Children model what they see and I modeled her! There is an informative and wonderful website; www.keeperofthehome.org in which Crystal Paine has written an article dated October 14, 2012 entitled, "How to Instill a Strong Work Ethic in Children From a Young Age." The article is as follows with excerpts regarding the chores:

"My parents wanted their children to leave home with three things: a deep love for God, integrity, and a strong work ethic. They were so motivated to teach us the value of hard work, that they set a goal to move out to the country by the time we were in our early teens.

With much prayer and effort, their goal was realized. And boy did we learn how to work! I have fond and not-so-fond memories of lots of back-breaking work: gardening for hours on end, dragging hoses all over the acreage to water the new trees we had planted, and spending much of the day on Friday taking care of the seven acres of the land that were planted in grass.

Truth be told, I wasn't always so thrilled at all the work they expected us to do. Sweating in the heat and developing sore muscles on a regular basis weren't necessarily what I'd considered fun. But looking back, I'm so thankful for the character I developed through all those hours of laboring in the hot Kansas sun.

The lessons in diligence and perseverance have been invaluable to me as a wife, mom, and business owner today. Truly, I believe one of the greatest gifts my parents gave me was instilling in me a strong work ethic from an early age. We want to do the same for our children and we're seeking to do this in the following five ways:

1) Model Hard Work Before Them

As has well been said, when it comes to raising children, "More is caught than taught". We can't expect our children to work hard, if they don't see us working hard.

This is something I still struggle with — especially when it comes to keeping my room clean. I'm not sure what it is, but while I tend to keep the main living areas of our home picked up and clean, our room and bathroom are the areas that often suffer.

I'm working on making it a habit to keep my room and bathroom clean, because it seems rather hypocritical for me to expect something of my children that I don't do well myself!

2) Remember That It Will Require More Effort Upfront

When teaching young children to work, it typically takes a lot of practice before they get it. Show them how to do a chore a few times. Then, work alongside them and help them do the chore. Finally, once you're really sure they've gotten it, let them do it on their own — and then be sure to inspect their work.

This takes patience and perseverance, but I promise it will pay off! I remember when I first started teaching my then 2-year-old and 4-year-old to clean the bathroom. It seemed like an exercise in futility at first, with no one really picking up on what I was wanting them to do.

But I kept at it week by week, and within a few months, they were working more independently. Nowadays, I just have to get the cleaning supplies down from the closet and they can pretty much do a great job on the bathroom all by themselves!

3) Give Age-Appropriate Chores

The last thing you want to do is frustrate your children by giving them chores that are too difficult for them! Start your children out with one or two simple chores and then gradually add more as they catch on and improve.

If you're not sure what age-appropriate chores might be for your children, you might find these chore lists helpful:

20 Chore Ideas for 7-Year-Olds

1. **Pick Up Their Room**— Make sure you show your child exactly what a clean room looks like. And if their room is really messy, I'd suggest working with them to clean it and giving them a few specific projects to work on at a time. Children at this age are often still learning the concept of staying on task, so you want to make sure you don't overwhelm them by giving them too many tasks to accomplish at once.

2. **Make Bed** — 7-year-olds can usually do a pretty good job of making their beds — especially if they are not sleeping on the top bunk of a bunk bed.

3. **Vacuum**

4. **Water Plants and Gardens** — A milk jug watering can is perfect for 7-year-olds. Just the right size — and it makes watering the plants and gardens fun!

5. **Sort, Start, Switch, Fold, and Put Away Laundry**

6. **Clip Coupons**

7. **Take Care of Pets**

8. **Dust/Wipe Down Surfaces** — 7-year-olds are great at cleaning baseboards, small floor areas, wiping down cupboards, or dusting surfaces. If you have a feather duster, they might have fun trying that out, too!

9. **Wipe Down Sink/Toilet** — Cleaning wipes work especially well for younger children to use. Or, you can spray some nontoxic cleaner onto a rag and let them wipe down the sink, toilet, bathtub, shower, or floor in the bathroom.

10. **Empty Trashes** — 7-year-olds can usually handle tying up the trash bag and hauling it out to the garage or back door — or even hoisting it into the dumpster.

11. Wipe Down Door Handles/Light Switches — Give your child a cleaning wipe or a damp rag and have them wipe down all the door handles. This is a favorite chore at our house!

12. Clear the Table – Teach your children to clear their plates after each meal.

13. Rinse Dishes/Load Dishwasher –A 7-year-old is usually old enough to stand on a stool at the kitchen sink and rinse non-breakable dishes (be sure to remove the knives and other sharp or dangerous objects before letting them do this). They can also help to load silverware, plastic cups, and other non-breakable dishes into the dishwasher.

14. Dry/Put Away Dishes — Children can also help with drying dishes (if you hand wash dishes) or putting dishes away from the dishwasher. We've found it seems easiest to start with silverware and then work up from there.

15. Simple Meal Prep --- Make 3-ingredient recipes, pop popcorn, make peanut butter and jelly sandwiches, and do a number of other simple meal prep things.

16. Set the Table — Teach your children how to set the table correctly from the time they are young–it's a skill many adults still don't know!

17. Sweep — 7-year-olds are usually capable of using a broom and dustpan. You may start your child out by having them, just sweep up your dirt pile and then teach them how to use the broom to sweep the whole floor.

18. Mop

19. Clean Out/Organize

20. Sorting — Sort books, DVDs, or other items and get them in order by kind, size, etc.

15 Chore Ideas for 4-Year-Olds

1. Pick Up Their Room

2. Vacuum

3. Water Plants

4. Fold Washcloths, Hand Towels, Underwear, & Other Small Items

5. Sort & Fold Socks — Sorting and folding socks can be a fun job for little people.

And you can teach matching, colors, and counting with it, too.

6. **Put Away Laundry**

7. **Dust/Wipe Down Surfaces**

8. **Wipe Down Sink/Toilet**

9. **Empty Trashes**

10. **Wipe Down Door Handles** — Give your child a cleaning wipe or a damp rag and have them wipe down all the door handles.

11. **Clear the Table**

12. **Rinse Dishes/Load Dishwasher**

13. **Simple Meal Prep**

14. **Set the Table**

15. **Mop**

10 Chore Ideas for Toddlers

::**Get Dressed** — They can also learn to put their dirty clothes in the hamper.

::Brush Teeth — with help from mom or dad to make sure they are thorough!

::Help Pick Up Room

::Water Plants — a watering can or small cup works great for this. Outdoor plants are best since toddlers tend to be a bit enthusiastic in their watering! ☺

::Fold Washcloths

::Put Away Laundry

::Pick Up Toys & Put Into Tub

::Dust — Give a toddler a sock to wear and let them dust all of the surfaces in a room.

::Wipe Down Sink/Toilet

::Empty Trashes — If you have small trashes in some rooms in your home, this is a perfect job for toddlers."

20

Expose Children To Reading....Early!

❦

When my children were younger, my son's favorite author was Roald Dahl and my daughter's favorite author was the late Judy Blume. I purposely exposed them to reading at an early age and read to them when they were in my womb.

Sidebar: When my children were babies and even as they got older.....I placed a tape recorder in the hall between the middle of both of their rooms and played the Bible on tape as they both slept. Children listen to music and can quickly remember the words......I purposely desired to get the "Word" in their spirits as they slept. You may be saying, "Crazy woman." Call me what you want, consequently, I have two wonderful, economically, self-sufficient, grown children who can stand on their own two feet with the help of God and for me, that is a major and significant accomplishment!

Surfing and googling the internet is fine, but libraries are still alive and well. Go to your nearby library and introduce your children to age appropriate books. Read to your toddlers. Carefully absorb and marinate it in your spirit the 10 benefits of reading to your child which the website below so eloquently points out: https://www.earlymoments. com/Promoting-Literacy-and-a-Love-of-Reading/ Why-Reading-to-Children-is-Important/

"We all know reading to our kids is a good thing—but are you familiar with the specific advantages your toddler or preschool-age child can receive by being exposed to the merits of reading? Below are some benefits that highlight the importance of reading to your child between the ages of two and five.

1. **"A stronger relationship with you. As** your child grows older, he'll be on the move—playing, running, and constantly exploring his environment. Snuggling up with a book lets the two of you slow down and recaptures that sweet, cuddly time you enjoyed when he was a baby. Instead of being seen as a chore or a task, reading will become a nurturing activity that will bring the two of you closer together.

2. **Academic excellence.** One of the primary benefits of reading to toddlers and pre-schoolers is a higher aptitude for learning in general. Numerous studies have shown that students who are exposed to reading before preschool are more likely to do well in all facets of formal education. After all, if a student struggles to put together words and sentences, how can he be expected to grasp the math, science, and social concepts, he'll be presented with when he begins elementary school?

3. **Basic speech skills.** Throughout toddler hood and preschool, your child is learning critical language and enunciation skills. By listening to you read One Fish Two Fish Red Fish Blue Fish, your child is reinforcing the basic sounds that form language. "Pretend reading"—when a toddler pages through a book with squeals and jabbers of delight—is a very important pre-literacy activity. As a preschooler, your child will likely begin sounding out words on his own.

4. **The basics of how to read a book.** Children aren't born with an innate knowl-edge that text is read from left to right, or that the words on a page are separate from the images. Essential pre-reading skills like these are among the major benefits of early reading.

5. **Better communication skills.** When you spend time reading to toddlers, they'll be much more likely to express themselves and relate to others in a healthy way. By witnessing the interactions between the characters in the books you read, as well as the contact with you during story time, your child is gaining valuable communication skills.

6. **Mastery of language.** Early reading for toddlers has been linked to a better grasp of the fundamentals of language as they approach school age.

7. **More logical thinking skills.** Another illustration of the importance of reading to children is their ability to grasp abstract concepts, apply logic in various scenarios, recognize cause and effect, and utilize good judgment. As your toddler or preschooler begins to relate the scenarios in books to what's happening in his own world, he'll become more excited about the stories you share.

8. **Acclamation to new experiences.** As your child approaches a major developmental milestone or a potentially stressful experience, sharing a relevant story is a great way to help ease the transition. For instance, if your little one is nervous about starting preschool, reading a story dealing

with this topic shows her that her anxiety is normal.

9. **Enhanced concentration and discipline.** Toddlers may initially squirm and become distracted during story time, but eventually they'll learn to stay put for the duration of the book. Along with reading comprehension comes a stronger self-discipline, longer attention span, and better memory retention, all of which will serve your child well when she enters school.

10. **The knowledge that reading is fun!** Early reading for toddlers helps them view books as an indulgence, not a chore. Kids who are exposed to reading are much more likely to choose books over video games, television, and other forms of entertainment as they grow older."

Books have the power to benefit toddlers and preschoolers in a myriad of ways. As a parent, reading to your child is one of the most important things you can do to prepare him with a foundation for academic excellence."

21

Questions and Answers

S everal questions and answers have been taken from Dr. James Dobson's book, "Dr. Dobson Answers your Questions" to help parents from various age groups because his teaching is in line with my teaching:

Q. "At times, I feel that I am overreacting to insignificant issues and at other times, I fail to respond to an act of deliberate defiance. How can I know when to ignore misbehavior and when to confront my child?

A. The ability to "read" your child's thoughts and feelings is a skill that can be learned by the mother and father who take the time to study the behavior of the kids. Ultimately, the key to competent parenthood is in being able to get behind the eyes of our child, seeing what he sees and feeling what he feels. When he is lonely, he needs your company. When he is defiant, he needs your help in controlling his impulses. When he is afraid, he needs the security of your embrace. When he is curious, he needs your patient instruction. When he is happy, he needs to share his laughter and joy with those he loves.

Thus, the parent who learns to comprehend his child's feelings is in a position to respond appropriately and meet the needs that are apparent. And at this point, raising healthy children becomes a highly developed art, requiring the greatest wisdom, patience, devotion and love that God has given to us. The Apostle Paul called the Christian life, a "reasonable service." We parents would do well to apply that same standard to the behavior of our children.

Q. I find it easier to say "no" to my children than to say "yes," even when I don't feel strongly about the permission they are seeking. I wonder why I automatically respond so negatively.

A. It is easy to fall into the habit of saying "no" to our kids.

"No, you can't go outside."
"No, you can't have a cookie."
"No, you can't use the telephone."
"No, you can't spend the night with a friend."

We parents could have answered affirmatively to all of these requests, but chose automatically to respond in the negative. Why? Because we didn't take time to stop and think about the consequences: because the activity could cause us more work or strain: because there could be danger in the request; because our children ask for a thousand favors a day and we find it convenient to refuse them all.

Q. My six year-old has suddenly become sassy and disrespectful in his manner at home. He told me to "buzz off" when I asked him to take out the trash, and he calls me names when he gets angry. I feel it is important to permit this emotional outlet, so I haven't suppressed it. Do you agree?

A. I couldn't disagree more strongly. Your son is aware of his sudden defiance, and he's waiting to see how far you will let him go. This kind of behavior, if unchecked, will continue to deteriorate day by day, producing a more profound disrespect with each encounter.

If you don't discourage it, you can expect some wild experiences during the adolescent years to come. Thus, the behavior for which punishment is most necessary is that involving a direct assault on the leadership and personhood of the parent (or teacher), especially when the child obviously knows he shouldn't be acting that way.

With regard to the ventilation of anger, it is possible to let a child express his strongest feelings without being insulting or disrespectful. A tearful charge, "You weren't fair with me and you embarrassed me in front of my friends, "should be accepted and responded to quietly and earnestly. But a parent should never permit a child to say, "You are so stupid and I wish you would leave me alone!" The first statement is a genuine expression of frustration based on a specific issue; the second is an attack on the dignity and authority of the parent. In my opinion, the latter is damaging to both generations and should be inhibited.

Q. I sense that this task of letting go is one of the most important responsibilities parents face.

A. You are right. If I were to list the five most critical objectives of parenting, this one would rest near the top: "Hold them close and let them go." Parents should be deeply involved in the lives of their young children, providing love, protection and authority. But when those children reach their late teens and early twenties, the cage door must be opened to the world outside.

That is the most frightening time of parenthood, particularly for Christian mothers and fathers who care deeply about the spiritual welfare of their families. How difficult it is to await an answer to the question, "Did I train them properly?" The tendency is to retain control in order to avoid hearing the wrong reply to that all-important question. Nevertheless, our sons and daughters are more likely to make proper choices when they do not have to rebel against our meddling interferences.

Let me emphasize the point by offering another phrase, which could easily have been one of King Solomon's Proverbs, although it does not appear in the Bible. It states, "If you love something, set it free. If it comes back to you, then it's yours. If it doesn't return, then it never was yours in the first place." This statement contains great wisdom. My point is that love demands freedom.

There comes a point where our record as parents is in the books, our training has been completed, and the moment of release has arrived. In summary, let me say that adolescence is not an easy time of life for either generation; in fact, it can be downright terrifying. But the key to surviving this emotional experience is to lay the proper foundation and then face it with courage.

Q. Do you think a child should be required to say, "Thank you" and "Please" around the house?

A. I sure do. Requiring these phrases is one method of reminding the child that this is not a "gimme-gimme" world. Even though his mother is cooking for him and buying for him and giving to him, he must assume a few attitudinal responsibilities in return. Appreciation must be taught and this instructional process begins with fundamental politeness at home.

Q. Must I act like a teenager myself in dress, language, tastes, and manner in order to show my adolescent that I understand him?

A. No. There is something disgusting about a thirty five-year-old adolescent has-been. It wasn't necessary for you to crawl on the floor and throw temper tantrums in order to understand your two-year old; likewise, you can reveal an empathy and acceptance of the teen years without becoming an anachronistic teenybopper yourself. In fact, the very reason for your adolescent's unique manner and style is to display an identity separate from yours. You'll turn him off quickly by invading his territory, leading him to conclude, "Mom tries so hard, but I wish she'd grow up!" Besides, he will still need an authority figure on occasion, and you've got the job!

Q. How can I teach my fourteen-year-old the value of money?

A. One good technique is to give him enough cash to meet a particular need, and then let him manage it. You can begin by offering a weekly food allowance to be spent in school. If he squanders the total on a weekend date, then it becomes his responsibility to either work for his lunches or go hungry. This is the cold reality he will face in later life, and it will not harm him to experience the lesson while still an adolescent.

I should indicate that this principle has been known to backfire occasionally. A physician friend of mine has four daughters and he provides each one with an annual clothing allowance when they turn twelve years of age. It then becomes the girls' responsibility to budget their money for the garments that will be needed throughout the year.

The last child to turn twelve, however, was not quite mature enough to handle the assignment. She celebrated her twelfth birthday by buying an expensive coat, which cut deeply into her available capital. The following spring, she exhausted her funds totally and wore shredded stockings, holey panties, and frayed dresses for the last three months of the year. It was difficult for her parents not to intervene, but they had the courage to let her learn this valuable lesson about money management. Perhaps your son or daughter has never learned the value of money because it comes too easily. Anything in abundant supply becomes rather valueless. I would suggest that you restrict the pipeline and maximize the responsibility required in all expenditures.

Q. How can I recognize the symptoms of marijuana use in my sixteen-year-old son?

A. According to Drug Abuse Central in San Antonio, Texas, the symptoms of marijuana use are as follows:

1. Diminished drive, reduced ambition.
2. Significant drop in the quality of schoolwork.
3. Reduced attention span.
4. Impaired communication skills.
5. Distinct lessening in social warmth; less care for the feelings of others.
6. Pale face, imprecise eye movements, and red eyes.
7. Neglect of personal appearance.
8. Inappropriate overreaction to mild criticism.

9. A change from active competitive interests to a more passive, withdrawn personality.
10. Association with friends who refuse to identify themselves or simply hang up if parents answer the phone.
11. An increased secretiveness about money or or the disappearance of money or valuables from the house."

Several questions and answers have been taken from Dr. Peter Favaro's book, entitled, "The Parent's Answer Book," to help parents from various age groups.

Q. My fifteen-month old was such a friendly, outgoing baby, but now she seems to have a negative reaction to almost anyone, but me. Her fearfulness is especially distressing to her grandparents, who want to interact with her; she just wants nothing to do with them. Is there anything wrong with her?

A. Kids go through two phases of separation anxiety....one phase occurs at around six to eight months, when infants show very clear preferences for their mothers or primary caregivers. The second phase, which is sometimes called stranger anxiety, peaks right around fourteen to eighteen months, and then declines from there. Until then, grandma and grandpa should be just a little more low-key. The good times are right around the corner.

Q. My husband has been a heavy drinker for the last fifteen years. We have two children, aged six and nine. I am concerned that living in the house with someone who is an alcoholic will make them more susceptible to developing a drinking problem themselves. What can I do about it?

A. You do not mention whether or not your husband has ever been in treatment for alcohol abuse, but it certainly seems as though he should be. Your children need to understand what it means to live in the same house with someone who has the disease of alcoholism. The best way to do this is to attend a few meetings of Alanon. Alanon is the branch of Alcoholics Anonymous that tends to the children and families of alcoholics. There is also a branch called Alateen, which is for the teenaged children of alcoholics. You can find out where the nearest Alanon meeting is by looking up Alcoholics Anonymous in either the white or yellow pages of your phone book and calling them. Please do this right away.

Q. Our twelve year old daughter will only listen to "heavy metal" music. We have heard that there are satanic messages embedded in the music that can influence children. Is this true?

A. Even if messages were subliminally placed in the music, they would not influence your child's behavior. Research on this subject does not indicate that subliminal messages influence behavior in any way. Think about it......if subliminal messages could influence us, advertisers would probably have us all acting like spend-happy zombies by now. As children reach their teen years, they are influenced more by their friends than by their parents, and that is where your concerns should lie. Musical preferences, sexual activity, and drug and alcohol abuse are all influenced by peers. That's why it is very important to communicate with your children when they are very young and more readily influenced by what you say."

The next two chapters are the voices of the author's daughter, April and son, Phillip from their perspectives.

22

Daughter's Perspective
❧

By: April K. Oliver

❝I have never met a woman who has endured so much as far as being a single, Christian parent. My mother was the type of mother who made you think you had it going on, even though we grew up in Southeast, Washington, D. C. We went to private school and she always kept us busy. Whether it was placing me in dance, tap, and jazz classes or going to church, it seemed like Monday-Sunday, church seemed to be our second home. We had a church family which was our foundation!

My mother is definitely speaking from experience as far as raising a child the right way. All the different tasks, such as spending intimate time with your children, treating your children with respect, and just being there to listen. She trained us to the best of her ability! The majority of the time, we train our children the way we were trained. No one gives you a handbook and says, "On your march, Get set, Go!" Training children is a day to day process that takes time. I am sure my mother is still learning from my brother and me and now from her grand-children.

In life, we get so wrapped up in ourselves that we tend to treat our children as if they are robots. We wake them up for school, make breakfast, take them to school, pick them up, make dinner, help them with their homework, give them a bath, and put them to bed. The same old routine, everyday and we hardly get a break in between, especially if you work and go to school.

There are some key things that I remember my mother doing, that were and are of importance. My mother never sent us to neighborhood schools. She either sent us to private schools or we went to school on Capitol Hill in Washington, D. C. near my Grandmother's home. This simply meant that our learning environment was hand-picked by our mother who was always concerned about my brother and my well-being! My mother never let us hang outside and that was because we were always going somewhere; swimming classes, tap dance, church functions, boys and girls club functions, bible study, tumbling classes, family events, the beach, parks, feeding the ducks! I can remember my mother taking us to different places and there would be young people cussing and talking loud. My mother would finally say, "Watch your mouth in front of my children." My mother became our protector when our father died on July 22, 1989.

The purpose of this book is to let you know that your child will stretch you until no end, but there is help. A church home is important; get your children involved in activities such as the choir, girl scouts, bible study, etc., also take time to see what is going on in your child's mind. They have feelings and a lot of times, they keep them bottled up. Remember your child is smart and knows your style; don't get "fooled." That means your child knows your strengths and your weaknesses.

Tough love is important; Louise Battle has shown this, numerous amounts of times without blinking an eye. "Get out", "No, No and No", and "Get out Again!" Remember, you are the parent; it is not the other way around, children will act like they are the parents. Any sign of weakness in you, your child will be the dictator, and you will not be preparing them to deal with this heartless world. Learn from someone who has played the cards she was dealt and won! Remember, "Life is short; cherish your children while they are here! Parents, please, I beg of you...drink honesty and consistency and pour it into the lives of your children."

23

Son's Perspective

By: Phillip A. Oliver

"The relationship between a child and a parent is one of the strongest bonds in the universe. A mother in many cases will risk her life for her child or even die. There are many sacrifices that parents have to make for their children in order to secure the best possible position for their child.

There are many situations in which the father is not in the same household or he is in a position where he is not capable of playing an active role in the child's life. My father was in my life until the age of 7, when he met his untimely death due to lung cancer by the age of 49. This situation grabbed my mother and put her into the throngs of single motherhood with 2 children to take care of.

My mother taught my sister and I core values that would be a primary reference for guidance in my life. The first principle was, Put God first, Respect others and be Mindful of the words that you speak, following the old adage, "If you don't have something good to say, don't say anything at all." I didn't know it at the time, but these principles would end up being more valuable than gold and the cornerstone of my manhood.

As a child, my mother would talk to me and if I did something terribly wrong, I would get a spanking as well. My mother was very soft spoken, but when she was serious, you would notice the firmness in her voice. There was a fear in me, but not based on a physical fear, it was the wisdom that was within the words and how she stated it, which would make me think; I know she is telling the truth and this is some advice that I should adhere to.

At the age of 16, however, I would let it go in one ear and right out the other. It would remain in the back of my mind, but I would still do things that I knew was wrong. I began drinking liquor excessively and smoking weed and cigarettes. I don't knock anyone for what they choose to do, but at that time, I felt that this is what I needed to do to become a man. As a young man with no definitive role model, we take different characteristics that we see in other people and apply it to our lives. My mother would talk to me about a man and how a man should behave, but I didn't accept it coming from a woman. I thought, "How can she tell me about what it takes to become a man?" These were very rough times in regards to my disobedience, but she never gave up on me!

One of the attributes that my mother has that I believe great parents have acquired, is the ability to have unwavering faith in your child and being supportive of them, regardless, of what is going on in their lives. Many parents want their child to finish *their* unfulfilled dreams, instead of allowing their children to create their own path. My mother taught me skills that I needed in order to survive in terms of how to read, write and communicate. She taught me how to cook, iron and created a work ethic in me by making me do chores around the house and outside as well. She taught me these things and many other skills that I would need to maneuver in life.

If you want your daughter to be a doctor and she becomes a painter, you should still be in her corner, 100%. If you want your son to be a lawyer and he becomes a sign language teacher, you can still stand proud as a parent; regardless of what my profession was, my mother sought for me to become a man of integrity and honesty. She conveyed to me that being a good man was the important part because before I could suc-ceed in any of those careers, I had to become a man first.

My mother knew that she could not raise a man, so she sought out different men that would take on the responsibility of teaching me. My brother, Victor Oliver stepped up to the plate and took me to his home on the weekends. He would play basketball with me and talk to me to make sure that I was doing the right thing. He genuinely showed me love and this made me feel that I was not alone. Contrary to what some people may think, young men need love from other men as well. A young boy needs love from his father and uncles and other men in his community. The love will be expressed differently than how a woman expresses herself, but this is how a boy confirms that he is a man; through his interactions with other men he aspires to and the validation he receives from them is important to his self worth and his journey to manhood.

One of my greatest mentors was Shaar Mustaf, who taught me about my African American history. He showed me how to dress and carry myself with confidence and integrity. There is not enough money to repay Mr. Mustaf for the values that he helped instill in me and to him, I am forever thankful. There were many times when I got suspended from school and he would take me in his office and have me watch, "The Eyes On The Prize" series. He would always talk calmly and he would not scream at me. I respected him greatly for this because many other men would scream at me when they were trying to correct me. He gave me respect, imparted guidance to me and gave me the tools that I needed to develop into a man.

Another mentor that my mother found was Porter Lawson. He took me into his home and to church with him. He gave me an example of how a man should develop spiritually. Many men have material things and have a great family, but they don't have a strong spiritual connection with God and this affects everything a man does. It even affects the faith that a man has in himself, because sometimes we give up on ourselves and we need that spiritual strength to keep us grounded. Mr. Lawson gave me sound advice and he ultimately wanted to see me strive and succeed. He took me to the basketball court because at that time, it was my favorite hobby. He would talk to me about some of the negative things that I was doing that were damaging the relationship between me and my mother. I am grateful for him taking the time out to teach me and show me how to develop not only into a man, but one with spiritual substance.

I watched my mother diligently look for men to mentor me. Some of them would step up to the plate and I would hear others tell her frankly, that they did not have the time. I appreciate my mother for going through this process. It taught me that a parent cannot do everything on their own and in many cases; they will have to enlist the help of others to help them achieve their goals. As a parent, you should never feel as though you are a failure because you can't be everything to your child.

The only thing you can do is try your best to raise them properly; give them the guidance and lessons that you have acquired over the years to enlighten them and help advance them into adulthood. Even the Bible says, "Train up a child in the way they should go and they will not depart from it." It doesn't mean that your child will not do things contrary to how you have raised them, because I have done many things to blaspheme the wisdom that my mother gave me. Some children have been disobedient and they will now spend the rest of their lives in prison; regardless of what your child's situation is, it is never too late for them to change or turn around from going in the wrong direction and head the right way. The most important lesson that my mother taught me was that, as a parent, your child has a destiny and a purpose. The parent may not know what it is and in many cases, the child doesn't even know because they are still trying to find themselves.

A parent's job is to be supportive and help facilitate that transition from ignorance to purpose. My mother <u>never</u> told me that I wouldn't be anything in life or stated that I was a failure, even when I was disappointed in myself. She only assured me that I had a purpose to fulfill and the only way I would be able to reach self-actualization, is if I had faith in myself and followed the principles in life that she taught me. My mother did not teach me how to be a man, but I have everlasting love for her because she helped me along the way in my journey to manhood!"

24

Understanding The Generations

Many parents are working hard at careers doing the best of what they know to do to take care of their families. I feel the need to explain in detail the X, Y and Z generations that we are dealing with to enable us to understand each other better. I am a member of the Baby Boomers and I believe that we need to understand each other as individuals, realizing that a person's family and social encounters will have a significant influence on decisions we make and can aid us in developing and improving quality relationships with each other.

I am using the valuable research of William J. Schroer, The Social Librarian in his website article at http://www.socialmarketing.org/news-letter/features/generation3.htm who explains it this way:

"Generation X
Born: 1966-1976
Coming of Age: 1988-1994
Age in 2004: 28 to 38
Current Population: 41 million

Sometimes referred to as the "lost" generation, this was the first generation of "latchkey" kids, exposed to lots of daycare and divorce. Known as the generation with the lowest voting participation rate of any generation, Gen Xers were quoted by Newsweek as "the generation that dropped out without ever turning on the news or tuning in to the social issues around them."

Gen X is often characterized by high levels of skepticism, "what's in it for me" attitudes and a reputation for some of the worst music to ever gain popularity. Now, moving into adult-hood William Morrow (Generations) cited the childhood divorce of many Gen Xers as "one of the most decisive experiences influencing how Gen Xers will shape their own families".

Gen Xers are arguably the best educated generation with 29% obtaining a bachelor's degree or higher (6% higher than the previous cohort). And, with that education and a growing maturity they are starting to form families with a higher level of caution and pragmatism than their parents demonstrated. Concerns run high over avoiding broken homes, kids growing up without a parent around and financial planning.

Generation Y, Echo Boomers or Millenniums
Born: 1977-1994
Coming of Age: 1998-2006
Age in 2004: 10 to 22
Current Population: 71 million

The largest cohort since the Baby Boomers, their high numbers reflect their births as that of their parent generation... the last of the Boomer I s and most of the Boomer II s. Gen Y kids are known as incredibly sophisticated, technology wise, immune to most traditional marketing and sales pitches...as they not only grew up with it all, they've seen it all and been exposed to it all since early childhood.

Gen Y members are much more racially and ethnically diverse and they are much more segmented as an audience aided by the rapid expansion in Cable TV channels, satellite radio, the Internet, e-zines, etc.

Gen Y are less brand loyal and the speed of the Internet has led the cohort to be similarly flexible and changing in its fashion, style consciousness and where and how it is communicated with.

Gen Y kids often raised in dual income or single parent families have been more involved in family purchases...everything from groceries to new cars. One in nine Gen Yers has a credit card co-signed by a parent.

Generation Z
Born: 1995-2012
Coming of Age: 2013-2020
Age in 2004: 0-9
Current Population: 23 million and growing rapidly

While we don't know much about Gen Z yet...we know a lot about the environment they are growing up in. This highly diverse environment will make the grade schools of the next generation the most diverse ever. Higher levels of technology will make significant inroads in academics allowing for customized instruction, data mining of student histories to enable pinpoint diagnostics and remediation or accelerated achievement opportunities.

Gen Z kids will grow up with a highly sophisticated media and computer environment and will be more Internet savvy and expert than their Gen Y forerunners.

Post-War Cohort
Born: 1928-1945
Coming of Age: 1946-1963
Age in 2004: 59 to 76
Current Population: 41 million (declining)

This generation had significant opportunities in jobs and education as the War ended and a post-war economic boom struck America. However, the growth in Cold War tensions, the potential for nuclear war and other never before seen threats led to levels of discomfort and uncertainty throughout the generation. Members of this group value security, comfort, and familiar, known activities and environments.

Boomers I or The Baby Boomers
Born: 1946-1954
Coming of Age: 1963-1972
Age in 2004: 50-58
Current Population: 33 million

For a long time, the Baby Boomers were defined as those born between 1945 and 1964. That would make the generation huge (71 million) and encompass people who were 20 years apart in age. It didn't compute to have those born in 1964 compared with those born in 1946. Life experiences were completely different. Attitudes, behaviors and society were vastly different. In effect, all the elements that help to define a cohort were violated by the broad span of years originally included in the concept of the Baby Boomers. The first Boomer segment is bounded by the Kennedy and Martin Luther King assassinations, the Civil Rights movements and the Vietnam War. Boomers I were in or protested the War. Boomers 2 or the Jones Generation missed the whole thing.

Boomers I or The Baby Boomers

Born: 1946-1954

Coming of Age: 1963-1972

Boomers I had good economic opportunities and was largely optimistic about the potential for America and their own lives, the Vietnam War notwithstanding.

Boomers II or Generation Jones

Born: 1955-1965

Coming of Age: 1973-1983

Age in 2004: 39 to 49

Current Population: 49 million

This first post-Watergate generation lost much of its trust in government and optimistic views the Boomers I maintained. Economic struggles including the oil embargo of 1979 reinforced a sense of "I'm out for me" and narcissism and a focus on self-help and skepticism over media and institutions is representative of attitudes of this cohort. While Boomers I had Vietnam, Boomers II had AIDS as part of their rites of passage.

The youngest members of the Boomer II generation, in fact, did not have the benefits of the Boomer I class as many of the best jobs, opportunities, housing etc., were taken by the larger and earlier group. Both Gen X and Boomer II s suffer from this long shadow cast by Boomers I."

25

Do You Know What Social Media Platform Your Teen Is Using?

⤞⤝

I read a very interesting article in the parenting section of www.tescoliving.com entitled, "How To Keep Your Kids Safe on Social Media" and it reads as follows:

"Whatever your feelings about social media, it is a fact of modern life. This isn't necessarily a bad thing. Social media can have a hugely positive impact on your child's confidence and opportunities, if you bear the following advice in mind.
"The most important thing that parents can do to keep their children safe from all online risks is to talk openly to them about their activities on the internet, and to make sure that they know what to

do if they see anything which makes them upset or uncomfortable," says Claire.

"Make sure they understand that the risks to their safety online are as real as face to face, and that people are not always who they say they are online."

"Children need to know that they should never give away personal details (address or telephone number), and that putting up images of themselves, which may seem like a bit of fun, is risky as they can't know who is looking at those pictures and if they may try to trace them."

"Once a photograph is online, there is no way of being sure it's ever completely removed, and the owner has no idea where it might end up - this forms part of an individual's digital footprint. Even sending an image in a private message is not secure. Children need to understand that the image may be viewed by someone other than the intended recipient.

Lynn Schreiber, founder of **Jump!** online magazine for kids, is a freelance social media consultant and mother of two. She suggests introducing your children first to social networks like Instagram and Pinterest, which are about sharing interests and images, and thus less likely to encourage bullying. Keeping a close eye on how a child works with these platforms – whether they can handle them appropriately – is a good way of judging whether they're ready for a Facebook or

Twitter account (bearing in mind that these have a minimum age requirement of 13 years)."

"As with anything, parents try to forbid their children, banning them from using social media is unlikely to prevent their accessing it.

If your child shows an interest in social media, it is far safer to allow him or her to use it under your supervision (by observing how he or she engages with others), than [risk their opening] a secret account which you cannot monitor," says Lynn. She explains that if you ban social media outright, your child may find a way to open an account and use it at school or at a friend's house instead. It's often better to allow an account (for which you have the password) and slowly give your child more autonomy over it as they prove they can use it responsibly."

"Used safely, social media can offer many benefits – for example, when online, children and young people can learn new things, get help with homework, express themselves creatively and connect with friends and family," says Claire Lilley.

Lynn Schreiber is also quick to point out the positive impact social media can have on a child's confidence: "Being active on social media exposes your child to receiving positive feedback from peers and strangers when they share a hobby or interest on a blog or social media platform, and it also allows them to connect with like-minded people and opportunities they might not have had otherwise."

I found a great website regarding social media which explains them so well. It is as follows: http://www.today.com/parents/moms-you-oughta-know-11-social-media-apps-teens-are-6C10833314

"Here's what parents need to know about the hottest social media platforms teens are using now.

Facebook

Your teenager is probably a Facebook user, but don't assume kids use this site the same way you do. Facebook is huge. It's a default. Not having a Facebook profile would be like not being listed in the phone book back in the olden days. Teens feel the need to maintain a profile there, even if they are not very active on the site. For best results on Facebook, do not engage your teen. Just lurk and collect information.

Instagram

This photo editing and sharing app is crazy popular with teenage girls who love their selfies. Instagram allows users to edit and post photos taken on their phone, and the images are publicly visible by default. Privacy settings are critical here because there are whole communities dedicated to displaying images of minors in sexually suggestive poses that are not technically pornography. Not to be paranoid, but innocent vacation pictures could end up in a forum for a pedophile.

Twitter

Twitter offers quick connection with anyone in the world. Users post updates in 140 characters or less. They can follow and be followed, as well as block other users from seeing what they post, but parents can also see what kids are posting without connecting, so long as they are not blocked. Because images can be posted, all the same dangers of Instagram apply. Remember, too, that if your teen doesn't want you to see their posts, they can simply start a new account and not tell you about it.

Pinterest

Pinterest organizes users around interests. Users create boards, which are like digital bulletin boards where favorite content is "pinned." It's incredibly popular because of its ease of use, ability to "save" content to look at later, and highly visual layout. Danger? Once a gathering place for home cooks and interior design aficionados, Pinterest has attracted its share of porn. However, your teen probably won't find it unless he or she is looking.

Vine

On Vine, users create and post 6-second videos, which are often also shared on Twitter and Facebook. Expect plenty of inappropriate content here including enough sex and drugs to earn the app a 17+ rating in the iTunes Store. With an unverified confirmation of the age requirement, users are ready to post video. Blocking who watches the video requires constant vigilance to make sure videos are not shown to strangers.

Reddit

Reddit users submit links or text, which are voted up or down by other users. Content is ranked to determine the post's position on the front page. All the content is organized into categories known as "sub-reddits." This site is more popular with boys, who are using the app less as a social network than as a source of news and as a search engine. The forum-like interaction means your teen can "talk" to anyone.

Tumblr

Tumblr enables blogging for those afflicted with a short attention span. Of course, teens love it. Photo, audio, and video posts are often re-shared from other sites with very little text. Tumblr's big attraction is the ability to create collections of media that quickly and powerfully express the poster's personality. Beware of the anorexia communities popular on Tumblr glorifying images of frighteningly thin young girls and women.

Kik

Kik is a smartphone messenger system where users send videos and images instead of text. Think emojis on steroids. Teens love meme and Kik allows them to search for and share images, memes and YouTube videos. Parents might be surprised to see some of the jokes their teens are sharing, but there is no unique danger here.

Snapchat

Snapchat allows users to send messages, primarily photos and videos that are destroyed seconds after they have been received. This service is marketed to teens with "capture the moment" messaging, and plays on its contrast to Facebook, which archives every post and pic for years. Snapchat's fleeting image feature offers users the illusion of anonymity, but screenshots can be taken. The biggest risk here is sending inappropriate content thinking, it can't be used against them. If your kids have the judgment of politicians, they could get into trouble.

Pheed

Pheed allows users to share all forms of digital content in 420 characters or less. Teens are the primary users of Pheed, which is one of the top apps in the iPhone store. Each user gets their own channel where they can post their content publicly or privately. In addition to the social media aspects like Facebook, Pheed is a full service broadcast medium. Users can share audio tracks and live broadcasts. Your teenager could conceivably live-stream every waking moment on Pheed. I think we've all seen that episode of "Law & Order." Users can also charge for access to the channel. A profit motive and under-developed judgment? What could possibly go wrong?

Wanelo

Wanelo -- which stands for "Want, need, love" -- is Instagram-meets-shopping and the dream app of many teenage girls. Users post images of and links to products, which are then bought, saved, tagged and shared by other users. When enough users tag a product, a store page is created. Users can follow stores and get updates when new products from those stores are posted. Wanelo is a wonderful tool to find out exactly what your 14-year-old daughter wants for her birthday. Serious threats to your bank balance here.

4Chan

4chan is a simple forum platform. Anyone can post images on bulletin boards, and anyone can comment. Similar to Reddit, the boards are dedicated to a variety of topics, but here users do not need to create an account to participate in the community. Anonymity can create extremely hostile environments online, so if your teenager is using 4chan, you'll want to have conversations about how to deal with virtual aggression.

It can seem overwhelming to keep up with teens' online lives, but take some comfort in knowing that yours is probably not active in all of these networks. As sophisticated as the technology is, and as fast as it changes, communicating with teenagers still comes down to real life conversations. And maybe a little snooping around on their phones. Which social media networks does your teen use?"

26

If These Were My Last Dying Words...

To My Children, Grand-Children, and future Great-Great Grand Children!

I could not imagine living a life without currently the six of you! Each of you in your own
unique ways has brought me joy and challenges
that have assisted in making me who I am. I am
a happy, fulfilled, grateful Woman, Mother and
Grandmother! I am grateful to God for allowing
me the opportunity to be all three. I do not take a
moment of it for granted.

There are many women who have and never
will experience child-bearing. I pray they adopt.
I enjoyed breast-feeding, helping with science
projects and term papers, (now I am helping the

grand-children do theirs), cooking you healthy meals that always include greens, (still doing that too) smile! I especially enjoy preparing special surprises for all of your birthdays. Each year preparing Christmas dinner, family fellowship and purchasing and wrapping presents for the entire family and my friends! All of your accomplishments keep me amazed, proud and humble. Phillip, CEO of his own business that provides jobs for family members and the community, giving young men and women the opportunity to learn a skill and trade. April, an Author, in her own right, having written two books and fastly approaching completing her third book. Both of you have graduated from college with degrees and your children and my four grand-children are on the way to accomplishing the same! I am at peace because none of you are in jail, in the cemetery at an early age and none are on the streets selling drugs or prostituting yourselves. You are _not_ walking around acting like you do not have a clue. Hallelujah!

It makes me happy to know that you know enough of your history and who you are in it to realize that your Ancestors and family members whom you KNOW who were enslaved, sacrificed and are still doing so, died so that you do not have to do any of the things I just mentioned above. All of you are a major part of why I work so hard! I intend to leave a legacy and I cannot die before I leave it......my way!

At my Home going service, when I transition to the next life, please take out the time at least 5-10 minutes to simply do a dance and praise the Lord in some way…for me! Now you know, there have been two cancelled funerals in my life…..the first was the deep depression I went into in 2001 and breast cancer in 2007, both were designed to take me out. Somebody, please say, "The Devil is Still a Liar" at my Home going service! I don't care about what time you have to be at the cemetery or that several people went overtime in giving their remarks, take out some time and give God a Hallelujah and praise dance. Phillip and April, I mean really cut the rug…you know how you both imitate me doing the "Holy Dance to the Lord." Do it, He is so worthy, so Great and so deserving!

Since your father passed, God has been my husband. You both know how I loved your father. I pray you two find and experience a love like that and that your children would see it, hear it and not settle for anything less! I have memories that have carried me through this life, most I have told you two about. When I start to tell you two some of the stories; you both tell me when I begin to get into the intimate parts of my life with your father, Frank, "Ma, too much information." It is always so fresh, as if it happened yesterday! Real *Love* and *Passion* are powerful and I have experienced them both at a higher dimension. I definitely pray that you two experience both. Please note, I never got it twisted: My relationship and the Presence of the Lord with me every morning, now, and forevermore, outshines any memory or fantasy I could ever imagine with your father or any man! I especially hope you experience that! Back to my original thought, God has been my husband since He took Frank. I believe that I could not have achieved more than I have achieved with a physical husband by my side, and that's the truth. I have not had the inevitable challenges and distractions that come with marriage, so it has enabled me to do God's work/ assignments coupled with accomplishing my own personal goals. My bucket list is so long....I am not really quite sure when I will have time to die! I do realize that the hairs on my head are numbered and I will be ready when that time comes.

After my transition to the Lord, Phillip and April: remember to stick with one another. Protect and love one another even more. Be there for one another, fellowship and call one another often. All you will have is each other, your children, your significant others and the rest of your family and friends. Eat breakfast, lunch or dinner together, *often.* Go to a movie together. Remember my perpetual prayer; the Be Be and Ce Ce Winans prayer for you two! I have watched Be Be and Ce Ce's relationship over the years....and I have always felt that they have an amazingly solid and lasting brother and sister relationship. I shared with the two of you that, that solidarity and endurance installed in your relationship is my prayer for the two of you. Do not let anyone come in the middle or cause chaos to your relationship....no one! I never raised you that way....to be separated and "at" each other. Teach my grand-children the same. They will continue to imitate what they see you two do and how you two cope! Mothers' Observation: "I have always felt that you have brilliant minds and told you both so! Both of you are different, but both of you are so much alike, kind, thoughtful and generous hearts, but stubborn in some areas!" Ask God to temper that stubbornness, it is not a negative quality; it becomes negative when it gets in the way of your relationships! COMPROMISE, sometimes! God is the glue that holds our family and any family together. Remember the plaque that has been visible in our home for many years stating, *"Choose you whom you will serve, as for me and my house, we will serve the Lord."* Joshua 24:15. I pray that you two will become more active in your churches, Union Temple Baptist Church and Zion Baptist Church. Ironic, you both chose Baptist Churches...I am just *thrilled* you chose church! Frankly, you have no other choice, but to serve God.....I won't see you again if you choose hell. Hell is not an option for any of my children or grand-children or great grandchildren or great-great grandchildren!

Love You to Life,
Your Mother, Grand-mother, Great Grand mother and Great-Great Grand mother.

The Blessings

April: (Daughter, 1st-born)

Frank and I named you April which means opening, peace, love. For us you meant, "Joy" because you were <u>our</u> firstborn and you bought us so much joy!

Woman of God, spread the joy, first to your children and then to other members of the family, and then to the world...not just joy, but over-the-top joy and happiness because in addition to me and your fathers' rough spots, tough lanes, challenging decisions and waiting on God... that's what we had....over-the-top joy!

Baby Girl, continue to write books, you also have an anointing to take care of the sick and down-trodden....God placed those tremendous and wonderful gifts in you! Always listen and follow the voice of God.

Phillip: (Son, 2nd Born)

Always listen and follow the voice of God. You are our peacemaker and full of wisdom baby. From a very young age you displayed those qualities. It is a "gift" directly from God and you use it well!

Continue to be a wise Man of God and pour out your wisdom over the people of God! Your daughters are blessed to have you as their father because of those gifts and Frank, bless his soul, is as proud of you as myself and your heavenly Father.

Precious: (Grand-daughter, 1st born)

I saw you born, such a miracle! You were named Precious because I was called Precious years ago by one person, your Uncle Ralph. He was right about that one, but you will be and be called Precious forever! Walk in it, own it, embrace it and treat people like you know who you are.....a Precious Woman of God.

At a very young age, you were the most appreciative little person I knew....over little things....you know the story....I have told it to you over and over. Become that person again. It is such a beautiful quality in you. You have so many talents and gifts.....take out the time to develop and use them ALL! Always listen and follow the voice of God.

Edward: (Grandson, 1st Born)

Always listen and follow the voice of God. I saw you born as well, so glad I was able to be there to watch another miracle! Please be there to watch the birth of all of your children and you will agree with me that it is an amazing miracle. You carry your grand-fathers' middle and last name. Frank means "free man."

Be you! Let no man, woman or child define you. You decide who you will become. Man of God, use your courage and faith. God gave it to you. Follow your heart, live out your dreams, goals and aspirations. Find out the purpose for which God manufactured and breathed breathe in your body and flow in it!

<u>Tatiyana:</u> (Grand-daughter, 2nd Born)

So alert and aware! You were a take charge person at a very young age. You do it well....now learn to use it wisely and it will take you far. Do not follow the crowd, you do not have to. Think for yourself...you have a great mind! You have the opportunity to continue to be "unique" and one of a kind......do so.

Use your "gift" of singing from God to light up and rock this world. Never forget to thank the One who gave you the gift. Woman of God, Always listen and follow the voice of God.

<u>Azaria:</u> (Grand-daughter, 3rd born)

Always listen and follow the voice of God. Your name means "Helped by God." How appropriate, we awaited your birth! It was so timely and much needed. As a baby, you smiled and laughed at the sight of us and at everything we said or did. It was so fun to make you laugh and you made us smile!

You are so curious, energetic and have a keen, watchful eye. You do not miss a beat! You will be a neat and detailed person who will love to laugh and make others laugh. We nick named you "Happy Feet." Little Lady of God, the world will be at your feet, but you <u>must</u> listen. Always listen and follow the voice of God.

To my step-children, Nadine, Yvette, Victor, Deon, Rodney and Derrick and their children and their children….Always listen and follow the voice of God.

27
Summary/Conclusions

Placing your "Faith" in Christian values in raising children is sure, regardless of what is going on in your children's lives. I am a very proud parent! These principles and values were in place before I was born. The secret of the Lord is with them that fear Him and He shall show them His covenant. Choose to have the audacity to believe God when your children's <u>now</u> behavior does not look like what God said it <u>would</u> be. It is a process and it will be.

We must practice discrimination in our faith and refuse to receive and nurture the curses, traps, and mess that are set before us as parents. Just as the promises were given to Abraham, we too, must believe that through our seed, all the nations of the earth shall be blessed. God is amazing and He is the main ingredient in Parenting By Faith!

This book has been written to ignite your faith in the promises that God has told us about our children, whether you know the promises or not. They have been stated throughout this book. Even if you know the promises, but your children's behavior and actions do not exhibit anything close to what God said and the promises seem dead to you, this book will assist you in believing that God does know and to trust His Word!

In my role of giving pastoral care to parents, adolescents, and children, if it were to be summed up into three points, they would be as follows:

1. Listen. Parents, children and teens all need to be listened to and need to know that they are important. They are very important to me, as the author of this book. I am always striving to understand all of them better. I care.
2. Motivate and pray. I have been called to make a difference in the lives of people to intervene, motivate and pray for families.
3. Refer only to reputable resources.

In conclusion, it is clear that parents need help. There is a critical need for the sharing of our faith with our children and to do it the way the Scriptures say. Merton and Strommen state it this way in their book, "Five Cries of Parents,"

"In the Judeo-Christian tradition, the command to teach one's children about God, go far back in the life of God's people. When Moses, the leader of the Israelites and giver of the Ten Commandments, spoke to his people about entering the Promised Land, he told them they were to keep alive the story of how God had led them out of slavery in Egypt.

They were to tell of how God promised to bless his people. Moses' instructions were clear: They were to teach these commands and promises to their children at home. How were they to accomplish this? Through conversation, symbol and ritual.

"You shall therefore, lay up these words of mine in your heart and in your soul, and you shall bind them as a sign upon your hand, and you shall teach them to your children, talking to them when you are sitting in your house, and when you are walking by the way, and when you lie down, and when you rise. And you shall write them upon the doorposts of your house and upon your gates, that your days and the days of your children may be multiplied in the land." Deuteronomy 11:18-21.

Understanding our children through spending time with them and knowing them, instituting the tips for single parents and being mindful of the developmental stages will place parents back in the drivers' seat.

Talk to other parents who are successful and talk to parents who you know have been unsuccessful. You can learn from both. Be cautious in listening to the advice of persons who have never trained a child or children of their own or for somebody else. They sometimes like to speculate and live and speak through inexperienced, idealistic lips. Most of all, establish an intimate relationship with the God who created and manufactured the little ones we call miracles when they first arrived in this world.

Faithful parents through history have followed these commands, using different methods, but always remembering what God has done for them, continuing to show His power and love. When you follow Jesus Christ and parent God's way using His Word, you raise the odds of your children following Jesus Christ. Please God by modeling Him and his laws and precepts in front of your children, saturate the daily environment and atmosphere with God's ways and commandments and give your children the incentive to please God also. Children often times, imitate what they see!

In the words of Paul J. Donahue, Ph. D, "Parenting Without Fear," "It takes a good deal of faith in them (our children) to let them be explorers, to trust that we have served them well and given them a firm home base and steady launching pad. If we can look back and see that we have worked hard to meet our goals as parents and recognize that we have done what we could to set them in good stead, we might be able to whisper to ourselves, "Good Luck, God speed, do your best."

The best way to begin to parent by faith if you have not already done so is to accept Jesus Christ as Lord of your life. The confessing of the following simple prayer places you on that path:

Heavenly Father, I believe that you sent your Son to die on the cross for me, I have said, done and thought some wrong things. Forgive me, come into my heart and take charge of my heart, life, mind, thoughts and body. Fill me with your Holy Spirit. Thank you for saving me!

Now go find a Bible believing church for you and your family where you can grow, be baptized and get stronger applying God's Word to your life! If you have said this prayer, but may have in some way messed up roy-ally or simply feel the need to reded-icate your life, say the above prayer and simply also say, Father, I give my heart, life, mind, thoughts and body to you all over again. Continue to mold and re-shape my life to glorify you! The angels in heaven are now shouting and so am I!

In conclusion and appropriately, the Words from the Greatest Book ever written, The Bible:

"No good tree bears bad fruit, nor does a bad tree bear good fruit. Each tree is recognized by its own fruit. People do not pick figs from thorn bushes, or grapes from briers. The good man brings good things out of the good stored up in his heart, and the evil man brings evil things out of the evil stored up in his heart. For out of the overflow of his heart his mouth speaks."

Luke 6:43-45 (NIV)

Author's Biography

Reverend Louise A. Battle was born and raised in Washington, D. C. more than a half a century ago. She heard the truth, fell in love with Jesus, believed it and then trusted Jesus Christ to be Lord and Savior of her life in July 1977 in Albuquerque, New Mexico at Shiloh Baptist Church. She was then baptized and joined her first Bible study. There has never been a desire in her to simply be "normal." Her desire is to leave a legacy for her family. She likes chasing lions! She and her late husband, Frank had their first child in Albuquerque, New Mexico. She does not pretend to be a guru on parenting and does not believe that she did everything right, but she knows what she knows.

Especially after the passing of Frank, she was always focused, loving, firm and thinking of creative ways to be a successful parent, training her two children to be independent thinkers to make the world a better place for themselves and others. She reached her goal and is humbled. It was not easy; she dedicated herself to working the plan to enable them both to become who they are! Did she shelter Phillip and April? Yes, with love and discipline! They were always "Stars" to her. She saw the talent and potential that God placed in both of them and she made sure they had the tools to grow. God gave her the plan for her children and she worked the plan!

She spent 4½ years in the U. S. Army and is presently in the "Army of the Lord." In July 1989, Reverend Battle responded to the call on her life to aid the homeless in New Mexico. She gave away or sold everything in her three-bedroom apartment in D. C., packed her bags and her two children and answered the call. Her husband had gone to be with the Lord, dying of lung cancer directly before she and her two children moved to New Mexico. She became a single parent and served as a Missionary in Albuquerque, New Mexico for 4 years to the homeless in a Ministry called "Noonday Ministry." It was there that God gave her a vision for a shelter/transitional home for single, homeless women and their children.

She graduated from the Howard University School of Business in 1974 with a Bachelor in Business Management and then returned to Howard University's School of Divinity and obtained a Masters of Arts degree in Religious Studies in 1997.

She worked for several years as a Social Service Assistant with the D. C. Child and Family Services in Washington, D. C. and assisted in teaching parenting classes to parents. She has trained two economically, independent and self-sufficient adult children, April and Phillip who know that they can stand on their own two feet with the help of God. Her son is the CEO of his own business; her daughter is a Clinical Technician and also the author of two books!

Reverend Battle is an anointed Spirit-Filled, Preacher-Teacher, dancer, singer, mother, cook and grandmother.

Her belief is that the anointing is needed to do everything....even vacuum her floors! She has traveled and divided God's Word doing workshops, and women's retreats in Greece, Washington, D. C., Maryland, Virginia, Delaware, Pennsylvania, Texas, New Mexico, Lagos and Benin City, Nigeria. Her messages are filled with truth, healing, restoration/reconciliation, wisdom, hope, instruction and deliverance!

She serves as an Associate Minister at Greater Mount Calvary Holy Church in Washington, D.C. in the Ministerial Alliance. Her covering are Shepherds; Arch Bishop Alfred A. Owens, Jr. and Co-Pastor Susie C. Owens. Her excellent counseling skills are valued in the Marriage Enrichment Ministry taking couples through pre-marital and post-marital counseling sessions.

She also serves as a Teacher in the Calvary Bible Institute.

She formerly presided over the Harriet's Children's monthly Friday Night, "Get Right" Services held at Greater Mt. Calvary Holy Church under the leadership of Reverend Barbara Reynolds. Reverend Battle has emerged as a 21st Century Esther and is the author of *No Longer Oppressed, Depressed and In a Mess, How To Hold On!* This book tells how God can loose your enslaved mind/body from a fornicating spirit and she has also authored, *"The Fight Is On!"* which tells about her journey with breast cancer and how she became a conqueror of the disease and proactive regarding her health!

She is the proud mother of April and Phillip and grand-mother of four; Precious, Edward, Tatiyana, and Azaria.

She comes highly qualified to declare and proclaim the Word of God because she has been clay in the Potter's hands. She has been broken, bruised, beat up on, hit upside the head, talked about, lied on, knocked down on the ground, ONLY, to get up and continue to praise Him who has loved her when she was faithless and ignorant of His presence, His mercy and His grace. She is on mission for her healer, deliverer and the great and wonderful mastermind Jesus Christ whom she knows has an undying love for her. The Spirit of the Lord is upon her!

**Other Books By
Reverend Louise A. Battle**

*"No Longer Oppressed, Depressed
and In a Mess, How To Hold On!"*

(Xulon Press, Inc., 2002)

and

"The Fight Is On"

(Xulon Press, Inc., 2010)

Space to Capture your Thoughts and Make Notes

_____

_____

_____

_____

_____

_____

_____

_____

_____

_____

_____

_____

_____

_____

_____

_____

_____

_____

_____

_____

_____

Space to Capture your Thoughts and Make Notes

Space to Capture your Thoughts and Make Notes

Space to Capture your Thoughts and Make Notes

I respect and appreciate your opinions. Please write me at the post office box in the front of the book or email me at Lbattlenolonger@hotmail. com and give me your comments or suggestions for my future parenting workshops, book signings and speaking engagements to better minister to parents.

Thank you!